SURFING THE RETIREMENT TSUNAMI

YOUR GUIDE TO STAYING AFLOAT AND RETIRING COMFORTABLY

By Keith Springer

D1617442

TABLE OF CONTENTS

PREFACE

If you can't explain what you're thinking or doing in plain

English, you're probably doing something wrong!

One thing I hope you will enjoy about reading my books is that I strive to write them in plain English, as if we are sitting side-by-side watching a ball game or a Hawaiian sunset, chatting casually over a beer or a nice glass of wine. I, for one, am sick of reading most things in the financial industry and saying to myself, *"What the hell is this guy talking about?"* or *"What a pompous windbag!?"* And I'm in the business!

For some reason, the authors of many investment books feel like they have to impress you with either the length of their words or the number of pages.

Not me, and not this book. I have been told that I have the ability for making even the most complicated subjects easy to understand. I learned that with my first book, *Facing Goliath – How to Triumph in the Dangerous Market Ahead,* and by writing a weekly client newsletter discussing the markets, the economy, tax law changes, and anything else that meant a damn to your money. So I figured I better get off my butt and lift my pen again to write this book. People deserve to read in plain English what is happening in our economy and what to do with their money, and that's what I've tried to deliver.

Don't get me wrong, it covers a lot of information on very complicated issues, but I have tried to bring them home just like I strive to do on my radio show. The complexity of some of the subject matter might make you scratch your head a few times (or perhaps curse under your breath in the chapters on economics and tax policy). However, as a whole, I think you'll find it interesting, useful and—most important— easy to follow. I want it to be a fun read, so if you're not having fun, tell me! I hope you enjoy reading it as much as I enjoyed writing it.

INTRODUCTION

WHAT IS YOUR BIGGEST FEAR?

Seriously, what is your biggest fear? That depends, of course, where you are in life. When I was a little kid, I would have dreams of falling. I would wake up in the middle of the night, shaking, damp from sweat, and indented in my bed about a foot deep as if I really did fall. Once, I swear I even felt a hand grasping my right forearm, but that's a story for another book.

As I grew older, those fears were naturally replaced with wanting to be liked in school, hoping to find love, and then, well, the fear of love. Maybe you had similar anxieties, or you are afraid of heights, alien abductions, or the most common, snakes. Whatever they were, I'm sure you have your own memories; with many you'd like to forge—just as I would.

However, as we grow older and our financial goals change from growth and accumulation of our assets to that of preservation and distribution, our concerns change with them. At this point, we move into the first two mature phases of life. The first phase encompass typically those from approximately 55-65, and then the second phase is made of those who are generally retired from about 65 on up. Although this book provides guidance and insight for all investors, its recommendations are
primarily for these two groups.

Something clicks inside us as we turn 50. Whether it's watching celebrities that we grew up with starting to die or the simple realization that we better get our act together if we don't want to work until the day we die that gets us concentrating on retirement. Studies consistently show that it is at this point in our lives that the fears of our younger years are replaced by worries about our health and running out of money in retirement. The good thing is that both of these worries can be overcome with proper planning and execution.

Once we have a few years of retirement under our belt, we enter the second phase, enjoying our golden years. Although we still worry about health and running out of money, we have pretty much dealt with these issues by now and have become comfortable with them. What keeps the second phase of retirees up at night is financial security for the surviving spouse and the legacy they would like to leave. One person usually made most of the money, oftentimes the man, and the other ran the house and raised the children. It's a model that has probably worked for many years, but eventually, one spouse drops out of the picture and the remaining partner doesn't know how to handle everything and needs help transitioning. This can be a very lonely and scary place in life, but proper planning can at least alleviate the financial concerns. With the stress of the money issues abated, it becomes much easier to continue to live the dream.

Lucky for me, I understood this years ago and started focusing my practice on providing retirement advice to these two segments of society. No one is more in need of a qualified retirement advisor. I also foresaw the economic tsunami that was barreling towards us, so I starting learning how to surf in order to be ready for it.

To truly understand what is going on in the minds of retirees, you need many years of experience, along with the same concerns. I don't mind admitting that I am scared to grow old. It's not the aging, per se, but the fear of losing my ability to do the things I like to do. Even though I feel great, I do not recognize the guy in the mirror each morning. I try my hardest not to grow old. I go to the gym six days a week (because going seven days hurts my bones too much), I take a handful of vitamins every day, and eat, even now drink, my greens. I even started doing Muay Thai with my trainer, Trey, at the age of 50. Certainly not something that is highly recommended, and I have the creaks, pops and cracks when I wake up to show for it.

Every day I battle with an angel on one shoulder and a devil on the other. If I could only give up my wine with dinner, my love of good Scotch, and my silly belief that peanut butter is ok to eat at 10 p.m. because it has protein in it, I would be Adonis. Although, as my son Josh tells me, "A great cigar needs to be accompanied by an equally remarkable Scotch, right?" He's studying to be the next financial retirement advisor guru, and his name is on the door, so I listen.

Although preparing financially is easier on the joints, it requires no less devotion. I began focusing my practice on retirement planning and becoming the nation's premier retirement advisor over a decade ago in order to make sure that my clients would have the proper tools to plan for that marvel retirement. In the mid 1990s, I discovered the correlation of demographics and the economy. It was then that I realized that 90 million baby boomers would be hitting their retirement years all at once. Ten thousand baby boomers a day are turning 65 years old. This trend started in 2011, and it won't end until 2033.

In simple terms—which I will go into in greater detail in Chapter 3—65 million Generation Xers are replacing the 90 million baby boomers. That's why our economy has been in the pickle that it's in: This smaller generation of consumers cannot possibly keep up with the same buying buyer. This slow growth and malaise economy will last until 2023, when the echo boomers, the kids of the baby boomers, start to hit their peak spending years. Only then will the economy turn around solidly and investing will be considered safe again. Until then, it's going to be very tough going, and if you are retired or in that retirement red-zone, you need to be extra careful of the dangers and start learning how to surf this impending retirement tsunami, watching out for the sharks along the way.

Millions of Americans are dashing towards their retirement with the promise that the rest of us are going to take care of them via Social Security and other entitlements. However, this assurance is doomed to fail. The government simply does not have the money. Therefore, it's up to you to put the pieces together in order to retire in the comfort and style you have always hoped and planned for.

It's not going to be easy, though. There is literally a tsunami of obstacles in your way. Company pensions are going by the wayside faster than rock stars enter rehab. If you do have a pension, you're one of the lucky ones. Most don't and going forward fewer will.

Social Security is not going to bail you out. I do think it will "survive," but certainly not in the form it is in now. Expect increased taxes on it and means testing to stealthily take it away from you if you are considered "rich," and I don't mean Rockefeller rich, either. I'm talking about an average couple that made a decent living, paid their fair share in taxes, and managed to save a little dough along the way.

The idea of selling your home for the big bucks, enough to live on in retirement, is gone and not coming back any time soon except, of course, if you are lucky enough to live in the Silicon Valley area.

Let's not forget that we are living longer. When I first started doing retirement planning some 30 years ago for my clients, we planned for one spouse to live to age 80. About 20 years ago that changed to 85, then to 90 and 95. Now, we have to plan an income stream that neither spouse can outlive to at least 100, or, more realistically, as long as there is breath in your body. With further advances in medicine and biotechnology, you can bet your booty that these numbers will only increase.

I discussed these issues in my first book, *Facing Goliath – How to Triumph in the Dangerous Market Ahead*. By understanding how demographics affect the economy and thus the financial markets, I was able to accurately forecast the 2008 market crash and bear market. In addition, I stood virtually alone in predicting deflation, which we are living with now, *not* inflation, as everyone had expected due to the government's stimulus and quantitative easing programs and the enormous printing of money that rivaled that of a Banana Republic. I'm proud to say I was right on this one too and my clients were prepared.

The good news is that your visions of retiring as you dreamed, hoped and deserve are still attainable. The bad news is that you are going to have to learn how to surf this gigantic retirement tsunami in order to get there.

Learning to surf at any age is tough, but doing so at age 50, 60 or 70 is a whole different ball game. On one hand, we're all supposed to be a lot smarter and wiser by this age, and life should be easier. On the other, we've all taken our lumps that life has dealt out and recovering from a mistake or a fall is a great deal harder and hurts a hell of a lot more.

Yet, that's where we find ourselves once we are retired or as we plan for it. You know what you need to do in order to create that life of luxury in your golden years, but are you prepared to do what it takes to get there?

Do you have the discipline and structure to save what's necessary and invest appropriately? Do you have the fortitude to live through the tough times? And do you have the patience to do the proper planning? Do you have the experience to apply the proper financial planning techniques to your portfolio and overall financial plan? And if you are working with someone, do they have the experience and expertise?

After all, true investment and retirement planning is a whole lot more than just investing your money. If you have the five or six hours a day to devote to studying the markets, economy, tax law, etc. and love doing it, then go for it! I've been professionally managing money for over 31 years and I can honestly say that if I wasn't in this business, I wouldn't do it. It's way too hard and emotional, and the chances of being wrong are much too great.

Just like any great team, you need a great coach; someone who knows how and when to play offense and when to play defense, someone who will keep your head in the game when the going gets tough, and someone to get you out of harm's way when you don't even see it coming. Someone who can put a winning game plan in place for you and create a customized retirement master plan for you and your family.

Never forget that true financial planning, and especially planning for retirement, is about a whole lot more than just what investments to buy. At this point in your life, you simply cannot replace this money. "How much can I make" quickly becomes, "How much can I lose," or afford to lose or, "How much do I want to lose?"

You need a plan that will create a retirement income stream that you cannot outlive. Taxes are increasingly becoming a problem because it's not what you make, it's what you keep that actually pays your living expenses. So, you must take advantage of often overlooked "retirement tax strategies." You need to employ a "marginal tax-distribution strategy" to make sure your assets are in the right place before you begin the "sequence of distribution" plan.

Even Social Security is overwhelming. For the average 62-year-old, there are 1,379 different options. That's ridiculous! Nevertheless, you need a "Social Security optimization analysis" and subsequent plan so you receive every nickel that you are entitled to. The difference can be $200,000 or more in lifetime income. That's real money.

At the center of your retirement master plan is your investment portfolio. Don't be confused by the terminology here. Your 401k plan is not a "retirement plan." It's an important account that is part of your plan, but that's it. Your plan is your comprehensive roadmap. Investment accounts—even things like 401ks—are just a tool to help you get there. Make sure you know when to play offense and when to play defense with your investment portfolio. Forget the old wives tales, like 100 minus your age should equal your stock weighting or the old 60/40, and whatever you do, stay clear of buy-and-hold. That's what I call "buy-and-hope"!

Your portfolio needs to be managed tactically at all times and always take the least risk possible to get the returns that you need, the importance of the planning. There are times to be all stocks and no bonds, all bonds and no stocks, and times to be in cash. Buy-and-hold will never go to cash, even when they know the market is going down. That's insane.

Some of the best trades I have ever executed were done during the crash in 2008 when I was buying the bonds of the companies that just announced they were to receive TARP funds. I figured if the government was getting into bed with these companies, they were a reasonably safe place to invest. I was picking up quality bonds at deep discounts with 8% - 15% yields; therefore, I was getting aggressive returns without any exposure to stocks and avoided devastating losses when everyone was getting crushed.

Playing defense is a little bit harder but even more critical for retirees. Knowing when to get out is extremely difficult, but knowing when to get back is even harder. Most investors who do manage to get out of the market, end up getting back in higher than when they sold. That's why you need a personalized written plan.

To protect our clients' assets, we use a revolutionary portfolio monitoring and asset-protection system called AssetLock™. This system monitors your investments every single day and helps protect your portfolio from devastating losses by establishing a predetermined downside based on the highest point the portfolio has ever reached, thus helping lock in gains. This allows us to manage our clients' assets with confidence. It's not a product or insurance; it is a proprietary process that is routinely attached to your portfolio.

Keep in mind that AssetLock™ is Plan B. Plan A is to make money. Plan B is in place in case everything goes to hell in a hand basket. And in such a case where AssetLock™ is triggered, we have a plan for systematically reentering the market by using the Recession Probability Index (RPI).

When investing in as dangerous of a market as this, make sure you have a plan for every contingency: A written plan. Don't just say you'll know when to get out and when to get back in again, because you won't. If you work with an advisor, make sure you ask what his plan is in writing. When a crisis emerges, markets respond drastically with no time to react rationally. Emotion sets in and mistakes happen. Avoid the headaches, heart attacks, and sleepless nights and be prepared.

Don't be surprised if your current advisor is not the one for you in the future, even if they have worked with you for many years. The person who helps you accumulate your wealth is quite often not the one to help you in that all-important next phase of life where accumulation turns into preservation and distribution. I have started working with folks who had their advisor or broker for 20 or 25 years and switched because they know they need somebody who understands the realities of retirees and appreciates what they are going through and what's going through their mind.

As a retirement wealth advisor, I am conservative by design. I have to be! When you work with people who are entering this phase of life, big mistakes cannot be undone. That doesn't mean making money on every trade or beating the market. Not by a long shot. It's about doing the proper planning so your goals are met with the least amount of risk possible, which translates into extra money in your pockets, fewer sleepless nights, and more happy marriages. It's the most rewarding job I know. One of my favorite things in the world is when a client looks at me and says "Thank you. Because of you, I can retire."

A qualified retirement advisor doesn't swing for the fences or put people in a "one-size-fits-all" financial plan. My holistic approach is distinctive in the industry, identifying not just clients' financial goals but their *life's* goals. Most of all, I believe in preparing for retirement and managing my clients' money in a very structured and disciplined way in order to get the very best returns with the least risk possible. This had me prepared for the dark days of 2008 as I was and still am for the bull market of 2009 to present.

Needless to say, planning for retirement is hard enough without the added peril of a dangerous economy, but that's where we are now. Retirees and those close are facing a veritable tsunami, and you either learn how to hold your breath for the next 5-8 years or you learn how to surf this retirement tsunami. So grab your surfboards and let's go for a ride!

CHAPTER 1

WHERE WERE YOU WHEN THE MARKET CRASHED?

For me, it feels like yesterday. The market was volatile but no one was ready for what we were about to endure. My special report, *An Economic Tsunami Lies Ahead – How to Prepare for This Perfect Storm,* which forecasted the massive demographic headwinds approaching and a major market decline, had been published just a few months earlier, but even I was surprised by how fast it occurred. The stock market is like a woman scorned: Watch out when she's mad!

It was vacation time. I had already begun taking defensive action, and I had a system in place if things got worse, as I always do, so I felt comfortable taking a little trip. When you work with people who can't afford big losses and don't have time or the stomach to make it back, you have to (what???)as well. Giving up some of the upside for protection on the downside is what it's all about once you hit your mid to late 50s, unless you've
got more than you need.

I was going diving with a group from Dolphin Scuba to go see Hammerhead sharks off Coco's Island in Costa Rica. Mike, the owner and my good friend, told me of this neat trick where you take a plastic water bottle on the dive with you and roll it between your hands. The sound is supposed whip the sharks into a frenzy. What silly kicks we divers get. As it turned out, the sharks were safer to be around than the market.

I had just started my trip and was in Arenal, Costa Rica on Monday, October 6, 2008: My first day. I had arrived at my hotel, bleary-eyed after a long red-eye flight. I had no idea what time it was. The iPhone (the original one) said 6 a.m., but there was no one to be seen, not even a waiter.

What I wouldn't have done for a cup of coffee right then, so much for getting away for a much needed holiday. I immediately started searching for a WiFi connection.

You might ask **why** I was frantically searching for a WiFi Internet connection in a Latin American resort hours before the business day normally started. To answer that, we have to go back in time almost seven years. After a fantastic six-year run in the stock market, it's easy to forget how terrifying the market can be. The good news is that I don't see another 2008-style meltdown any time soon. But the bad news is that the U.S. market is looking a little on the expensive side, and the market is no longer priced to deliver high returns. The easy money has already been made. This is not to say that I don't expect to make money in the years ahead; I most certainly do. But I firmly believe that in order to make that happen, we need to take a more flexible and tactical approach to investing. In the second half of this decade, it will pay to stay nimble.

I don't want to dwell on the past, but there are a lot of important lessons to be learned from the 2008 meltdown. In a lot of ways, it really did change the rules of the game. My goal here is to teach you these new rules so that we can both earn respectable returns without the risk of losses you can't bare for the next 5-7 years until things get better.

Let's go back in time to those scary days of late 2008. We're in the middle of the most tumultuous period the stock market has seen since the Great Depression. Just three weeks before, the unthinkable had happened: Lehman Brothers, the 158-year-old stalwart of the financial world collapsed and declared bankruptcy. I must admit, that weekend had been one of the most electrifying times in my 25+ years as a wealth advisor, and I remember the Sunday morning of September 14th as if it were yesterday. I was entertaining friends in the backyard and was a rude host that day, running back and forth from my computer to my guests, wondering who

—if anyone—was going to rescue Lehman.

Sometime that afternoon, I was taken aback by news that I simply wouldn't have believed a year earlier. Merrill Lynch was in talks to be bought out by Bank of America. That could only mean one thing: They were going down, right then and there, and the immediacy indicated they couldn't open for business on Monday. They lacked the funds to continue operations. I was literally shaking with both shock and excitement, as if expecting a visit from an evil Santa Claus. My career had started with Merrill in 1985, and since then, I thought of Merrill as being invincible. Frankly, watching it collapse was terrifying. It shattered many of the remaining illusions that I had carried with me from those early days. What a different world it was than when I started. Ronald Reagan was president, and I watched the Dow cross 1,300! The biggest bull market in world history was in its infancy.

I knew it was going to be a rough few years, and I was prepared and needed to get away for a nice holiday to clear my head. This trip to Costa Rica had been planned for almost two years and although my portfolios were ready, nothing prepares you mentally for a crash, even if you think you are.

As I awaited that cup of coffee from Juan, an attentive waiter in the Arenal Volcano Hotel lobby, I flipped on my laptop and once again felt that twisting sensation in the pit of my stomach. The Dow was down some 800 points! Oh my God, that meteor that I thought had veered from its course was now once again hurtling toward Earth, only this time it was closer than ever. I hadn't avoided Armageddon; it was happening before my very eyes!

With the beautiful, vast and serene Arenal Volcano to one side and the mushroom cloud emanating from my computer on the other, I couldn't help but notice the eerie difference between the tranquility of my surroundings and the sense of panic and hysteria over the impending destruction of the world's financial foundation. It was surreal and felt like being snatched from your mother's arms as a child and then thrown to the wolves.

The world was crumbling, the financial world at least, and although I had expected such a decline eventually and was confident that I was prepared, I kept thinking that there was more that I should have done. I had written my *Economic Tsunami* report detailing how the economy would unravel just a few months before, but I must admit that the timing caught me by surprise. Knowing that calamity is coming and living through it are two entirely different things.

Months before, I witnessed the unthinkable: The collapse of Bear Stearns, one of the biggest and baddest investment banks on the planet. They had been considered more than solvent just a few days before. But as the bank's counterparties suddenly lost faith in its ability to honor its commitments, the government was forced to broker a deal whereby JP Morgan Chase would absorb Bear. Just like that, a major Wall Street institution—a former pillar of strength and stability— went up in a puff of smoke. If it could happen to them, it could happen to anyone. Little did we know, Bear's collapse would set off a chain reaction that would eventually bring the international financial system— and global capitalism itself—to the brink of destruction in October 2008.

And, so, that is how I found myself in a hotel lobby that morning, attempting to deal with the implications of this meltdown for my clients from the wilds of Costa Rica. Over the several tense days that followed, I did my best to calm client fears while continuously reevaluating my strategy to not only protect my clients' money, but to take advantage of the situation. After all, people weren't paying me to sit like a deer in the headlights. As a wealth advisor, I am expected to make money.

To keep my head clear, I managed to toss in a little adventure: zip-lining through the Monteverde rain forest, repelling through the 100 ft. Fortuna waterfalls, and rafting down the class 4 and 5 rapids of the Toro River with the Howler monkeys, well, howling at the top of their lungs. It was as though they were laughing at me and my feeble attempt to escape reality, even if for just a moment. I must admit, had it not been for such audacious activities that instill the fear of death in you, I would have probably gone insane.

I managed to unwind a little by enjoying some of the excellent locally

made cigars during the daily afternoon downpours, giving me time
to ponder. I was fortunate enough to have had a private tour of Don
Benigno's cigar factory at the beginning of our trip, highlighted by a visit
from Don Benigno himself. He had a trick he liked to show off where he
would stand one of his cigars on its ash. Because Don Benigno's cigars
are rolled so perfectly, they would
stand up on their own!

As we sat in his courtyard, sipping espresso and enjoying his finest
Robusto while trying desperately to understand each other in my
broken Spanish, I couldn't help but feel jealous at his innocent
obliviousness to the meteor
that was hurtling toward Earth, mere seconds from impact.

I managed to finish my wonderful journey after Scuba Diving with the
Hammerheads off Coco's Island, while racking up a satellite phone
bill the size of a mortgage payment. Although sad at the end of my
trip, I needed to be home to witness the carnage for myself and to
at least have the feeling of being in control again. As I finally got off
the plane in Sacramento, I half expected to see people screaming,
buildings burning, and smoke billowing from the sky. Of course,
that's not what was going on at all. The "real" world appeared to
be completely unconcerned about the precarious cracks in the
foundation of our financial system. It would be several months until
the average man on the street would feel the effects. Lucky stiff!

I realized a very important reality that month: **The laws for
investing had changed.** No longer could you just buy blue chip
stocks or a mutual fund and sit back and watch it go up like we did
in the 80s and 90s. No longer could we buy the stock of a household
name and hold it forever like our grandparents did. No. Buy-and-hold
was dead, having turned into *buy-and-hope*. And complicating things
further was the loosest monetary policy in the history of the United
States. The Fed first lowered short-term rates to 0%. And when that
wasn't enough, they gave us multiple rounds of quantitative easing.
Talk about a game changer. Momentum investors found that the only
thing that seemed to matter in the direction of the stock market was

Fed policy. And value investors found their valuation models skewed by artificially low rates. For perhaps the first time in the history of the U.S. stock market, all of the established models were rendered close to useless. Given these complications, I realized quickly that for the foreseeable future, I'd have to take a tactical approach.

And after seven years of post-crisis bull market, the question I hear most often is "Where do we go from here?"

After taking heavy losses in 2008, a lot of investors got out of the market, missing most of the gains. But even most of those investors who rode out the storm have a massive gap in their investing timeline. It wasn't until 2013 that the S&P 500 finally pushed through its old year 2000 highs (**Figure 1.1**). That's 13 years of zero returns, and I haven't said a word about inflation. Taking inflation into account, we're still well below the old 2000 highs. And during the pits of the 2008 meltdown, the selling not only erased five years' worth of gains, it took the S&P 500 down to levels first seen in 1996.

13 years is a ridiculously long time to go without a positive return. Some advisors, brokers and bankers have the gall to say that it's ok, because "over the long run, the market always goes up." Not me. That's just plain lunacy. Even worse for these poor schmucks is that these lost years happened at a devastating time for investors in the peak earning years of their late 40s and 50s. For many of these investors, retirement depended on their ability to earn respectable returns during those crucial years. Today, many have had to postpone retirement indefinitely or to accept a retirement lifestyle far more modest than they planned. Dreams of sailing around the world or simply spending more time with the grandkids would have to remain dreams. Many will even have to work for the rest of their lives.

Of course, many Americans have a significant portion of their wealth tied up in the equity in their home. The model for prior generations was to sell their large suburban homes that had appreciated in value over the years and to use the proceeds to help fund a comfortable retirement. A retiring couple could sell their suburban home for, say, $500,000, whereas the new retirement home might only cost

Figure 1.1: S&P 500 Index

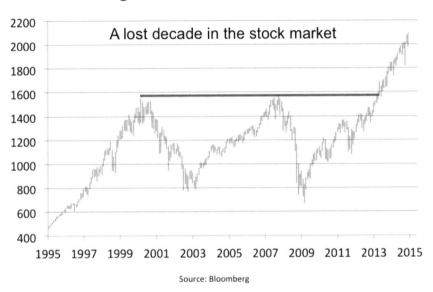

Source: Bloomberg

Figure 1.2: Change in Debt Outstanding

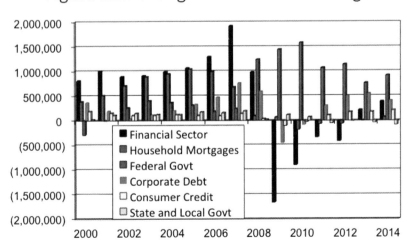

Source: Federal Reserve Flow of Funds Report (FRB Z1)

$250,000. The difference could be used to fund an annuity. At current market rates, $250,000 would generate roughly $1,200 per month to a hypothetical husband and wife aged 62. Many would-be retirees budgeted this income to supplement Social Security and their other pensions and investments.

Well, this is under threat too. Home prices have recovered nicely over the past few years, but these gains are precarious. House prices are affected by mortgage rates. The lower the mortgage rate, the cheaper the monthly payment. Well, mortgage rates are near all-time lows right now. If mortgage rates rise to something closer to their long-term averages, monthly payments get a lot less affordable. This is why Bernanke and Yellen kept their "QE infinity" bond buying program going as long as they did. Both feared what might happen to the housing market in the event of a mortgage rate spike. Meanwhile, the aggressiveness of the federal government's response has caused government debt to spiral out of control. Currently, the total federal debt stands at a whopping $18 trillion. Debts, of course, have to be repaid. And in the private sector, we are starting to see this. Total debt outstanding by individuals and corporations is actually shrinking (**Figure 1.2**). In fact, the private sector is paying off debts faster than the government is accruing them. Though this process of deleveraging is essential to the long-term health of the country, it comes at a heavy cost. Every dollar used to repay debt is a dollar that cannot be spent in the economy.

What is done is done. We cannot change the past, and the question remains, "Where do we go from here?"

This is the question I intend to answer in the pages that follow, and the outlook is mixed. Not "bad," mind you, just mixed.

There is good news and there is bad news. The good news is that after reading this book, you will be prepared. The bad news is that I expect there to be some pretty serious ups and downs in the next five to seven years. In America's borrowing binge, private-sector and government debts simply got out of control. Debt is a way of bringing future consumption into the present. A dollar borrowed to use today is a dollar that is unavailable to be spent tomorrow. That is, unless you intend to borrow another dollar. Of course, there are limits to the amount of borrowing that can be done. The next several years will be marked by Americans paying down their debts. The result, to the surprise of many, absent government intervention through stimulus, will likely be a prolonged period of deflation or at the very least extremely low inflation.

As I mentioned briefly, demographics play a large role here. The Baby Boomer generation has reached a critical threshold. The bulk of the generation has now passed its peak years for spending growth. They have now reached the stage of their lives marked by saving, not spending. As the biggest and richest generation in history, this retrenchment by the Boomers will be a major headwind for the U.S. economy. This is a line of research and analysis that was pioneered by Harry S. Dent, Jr. Harry's contribution to the industry's understanding of how demographics impact the economy has been immeasurable and his research served as a cornerstone of this work.

There are definitely some positive trends that we can follow. The Echo Boomers, the kids of the original Baby Boomers, are now entering the family-formation stage themselves. They got a late start, given that they started their careers during the worst economy in a generation. But I expect them to make up for lost time. They will also one day enter their peak spending stages of life and create the next wave of aggregate demand the economy needs. These new American families represent the future for the country, and the future will indeed be bright—once we get through the current hell to pay from previous excesses.

Outside of the United States, we are witnessing economic miracles happening in the emerging market countries of Asia and Latin America. Millions of people who formerly toiled as low-wage laborers are entering the new global middle class every year. The emergence of this new middle class is the single biggest growth story of the next 20 years.

Even in the crisis-plagued United States, great opportunities exist for investors to repair their balance sheets and fund their retirements. Many of America's best companies are trading at bargain prices and pay cash dividends that are higher than 30-year bond yields. Even during a prolonged economic slump, a portfolio of high-yielding blue chips with a proven track record of surviving and prospering in difficult conditions offers the potential for respectable returns. However, as you will learn, it's not always the obvious blue chips with their mediocre dividends that provide the best success, but identifying that niche marketplace of undervalued stocks that pay extraordinary dividends.

In short, we are looking at several difficult years ahead. But with proper planning and tactical portfolio management, this is not something that should concern us. Uncertainty creates opportunity. As my good friend Tom once said, "Never let a good crisis go to waste!"

In the pages that follow, I intend to explain how we arrived at where we are today and how we as investors can prosper, regardless of which direction the economy takes.

CHAPTER 2:

WHAT A LONG, STRANGE TRIP IT'S BEEN

There is no doubt that the last decade has been a wild ride. It's been a rollercoaster with none of the flat parts to calm your stomach. Who needs moderation when you can triple your money in a few short years, only to give it all back in the matter of months, over and over again…?

Of course, if you're past your risk-taking years, that's a lot less appealing. I have met with hundreds of people who were there; who had all the money they needed. They had won the game as long as they weren't stupid with their money, only to take more risk than they needed and lose their financial security. If you are simply riding a wave up and down, you are missing the point of surfing. Let's go back in time and review the boom, the bust, and the new boom that followed. Home prices nationwide peaked in early 2006 and are still nowhere near their old highs in most cities (**Figure 2.1**). The unemployment rate shot up to over 10%, a level it hadn't seen since 1982, and has slowly dribbled down over the past five years. It's now under 6% or close to the *highs* it reached after the early 2000's technology bust. Stop and think about that for a minute. After steadily falling for five years, the unemployment rate is just now reaching the highs of the previous recession. (**Figure 2.2**). It still has a lot of falling to do in order to reach anything close to full employment. And again, this is after *five years*.

Those readers familiar with the legal system have no doubt heard the expression "proximate cause." It tends to come up most frequently in lawsuits. The proximate cause is the cause closest to an event. There may have been plenty of contributing factors along the way, but the proximate cause is the last one.

The proximate cause for the Great Recession was the credit crisis that began in late 2007 when the banks first began to acknowledge their losses on their subprime mortgage portfolios. The crisis accelerated in 2008 with the failures of Bear Stearns and Lehman Brothers. By the time the crisis abated in early 2009, the damage was done. The credit system was impaired, Americans collectively lost hundreds of billions of dollars of accumulated wealth, and consumer confidence was shattered.

Fast forward to the present and not much fundamentally has changed. A steady stream of government stimulus has at least given the illusion of stability, and Americans are no longer paralyzed by anxiety—yet, they are not exactly oozing confidence either. They are starting to spend money again, slowly and in fits and starts. But the old swagger is long gone, as is the willingness to take risk.

A bona fide credit crisis is a crisis of confidence that results in a destabilizing lack of liquidity. But in layman's terms what does that actually *mean*? Where does the liquidity "go" at the onset of a crisis? After all, can money just disappear?

In the banks of the 1800s and early 1900s, the mechanics were fairly simple. For any number of reasons, real or imagined, depositors would lose faith in a bank as the steward of their savings and would demand their money back—in cold, hard cash. Of course, banks only keep a small fraction of customer deposits on hand and loan out the rest. So, when demand for deposited funds exceeds the cash on hand, the bank is forced to call in loans, and the borrowers have to scramble to find other sources of funding. Otherwise, they have to liquidate their assets in order to pay back their debts. Of course, buyers for those assets would be scarce because the financing to make a sale possible would be unavailable—after all, if the bank is calling in existing loans, it doesn't have the cash on hand to facilitate the deal. The result is a downward spiral of fear and panic and, typically, a severe bear market, recession and downward pressure on prices.

The Federal Reserve was created in 1913 to prevent these kinds of bank runs. Going forward, banks would have the ability to take short-

Figure 2.1: Case Shiller 20-City Home Price Index

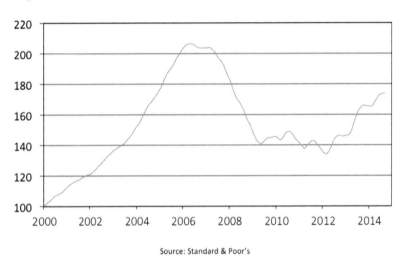

Source: Standard & Poor's

Figure 2.2: Unemployment Rate

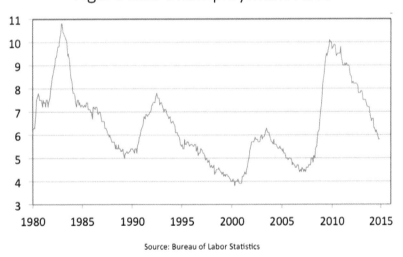

Source: Bureau of Labor Statistics

term borrowings from the Fed in order to satisfy immediate liquidity needs. In other words, the Fed can act like a giant pawn shop, offering emergency loans as needed. And like a pawn shop might take your watch as a security deposit, the Fed takes high-quality bonds from the borrowing bank's portfolio as collateral for the loan.

Furthermore, by regulating the Fed funds rate, the Fed can lower the cost of funds for short-term loans between banks. Lowering the Fed funds rate had the effect of injecting liquidity into the system. Banks had no reason to fear systemic collapse and could thus lend freely to one another. We could all have confidence in the system.

So what went wrong in 2007 and 2008? Why, for all intents and purposes, did we have an old-school crisis of confidence? Where did the liquidity go? And how can we avoid getting sucked into something like this again?

For answers, we turn to Paul McCulley, Managing Director of Pimco, the world's largest bond management firm. Writing for the CFA Institute, Mr. McCulley says:

> My simple thesis is that **liquidity is a state of mind.** In the current market and talk of a liquidity crunch, investors are asking, where did the liquidity go? This question reflects the concept taught in basic economics that the money stock is the liquidity in the market, which creates the concept of liquidity as a pool of money. It is a very bank-centric concept of liquidity; the U.S. Federal Reserve (Fed) injects and withdraws liquidity, and the banks transform liquidity into deposits and loans. Thus, investors think of liquidity as a pool of money, and during a downturn, they wonder where the liquidity went.
>
> **My answer is that liquidity is not a fixed pool of money but, rather, a state of mind and, in particular, a state of mind regarding risk.** Liquidity is the result of the appetite of investors to underwrite risk and the appetite of savers to provide leverage to investors who want to underwrite risk. **The greater the risk appetite, the greater the liquidity, and vice versa.** Put

another way, liquidity is the joining or separating of two states of mind—a leveraged investor who wants to underwrite risk and an unleveraged saver who does not want to take risk and who is the source of liquidity to the levered investor. The alignment or misalignment of the two investors determines the abundance or shortage of liquidity.

Financial markets and the capitalist economy are driven by what John Maynard Keynes called "animal spirits," which, if you have ever seen the hyperactive trading floor of the New York Stock Exchange, needs no further explanation. Unfortunately, the instinct that drives these animal spirits can quickly turn to fear, which has largely been the case since 2007. We're starting to see the animal spirits return to the stock market. *Starting*. But it's been a long time coming.

Speculative booms generally end in deflationary busts, and the epicenter of the speculation typically endures a long period of contraction and stagnation as the excesses of the boom are slowly absorbed and worked off. In the case of the subprime mortgage crisis, a speculative house of cards was built around a single premise: that home prices would always rise, thus making mortgage lending (even subprime, ARMs, "no doc," etc. a near riskless business, particularly if mortgages were properly bundled to diversify the risk.

There is a demographic story here as well. The boom in housing that made all of this possible was a result of the Baby Boomer trade-up cycle, in which successful Boomers used their hard-earned spending power to buy the homes of their dreams. Once the boom reached the speculative bubble stage, the buying spread far beyond the financially sound core of middle-class Boomers to lower-income and younger marginal buyers. Finally, when mania set in, would-be homeowners were afraid of being left behind by their peers if they didn't buy. After they watched their home-owning neighbors score enormous paper gains on their properties, they felt, in the desperate logic that dominates a mania that they couldn't afford not to buy. (By the way, I'm starting to see some of this same mentality among professional money managers and wealth advisors that had their clients mostly out of stocks these past six years. It's a dangerous, reckless mentality so watch out for it!)

When adjustable rate mortgages began to reset and marginal buyers were unable to continue paying or to refinance at the then prevailing mortgage rate, the default rate on mortgages started to soar. Furthermore, the higher interest rates caused the value of virtually all long-term bonds to fall, included mortgage bonds and the alphabet soup of derivatives based on them (MBS, CMS, etc.) As homes and the mortgages written on those homes continued to fall in value, no bank or broker was willing to accept mortgage bonds on derivatives as collateral for new loans. It would be like going to a pawnshop for business as usual and discovering that the pawnshop owner abruptly stopped accepting watches like the one you intended to pawn as collateral.

When "Bank A" gets scared and refuses to accept the bonds as collateral, "Bank B" gets scared and follows suit. Suddenly, there are no takers in the marketplace. The watch on your wrist, whether a Rolex or a Timex, is suddenly viewed as worthless trash that no pawnbroker would lend against.

This brings up another arcane term that wreaked havoc during the crisis: "mark to market." Hedge funds, investment banks, and lenders have to carry the assets (mortgage loans) on their books at "fair market value," meaning the prevailing price. The problem is, when there are no buyers, there is no market price to be marked to, and so the price drops precipitously. Suddenly, the mortgage assets held in these companies' portfolios are worth considerably less or nothing at all, but the money that they borrowed to fund those assets still has to be paid back. In many cases, these "mark to market" losses might only be temporary. But that doesn't stop, say, a company from being in technical default and from being forced to sell assets at a fire-sale price in order to meet short-term liabilities. This further reduces the price, which causes more fire sale selling from others, causing the downward spiral that we witnessed during the crisis. So where does

Figure 2.3: Federal Reserve Balance Sheet

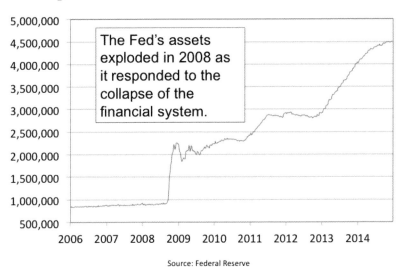

Source: Federal Reserve

Figure 2.4: Adjusted Monetary Base

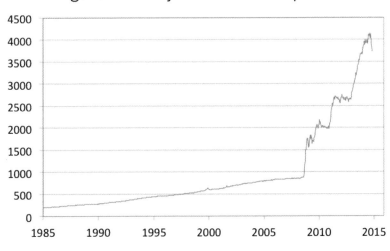

Source: Federal Reserve Bank of St. Louis

it all end?

The move by the Federal Reserve to accept "nontraditional" collateral on loans (e.g., mortgage assets) and to massively expand its balance sheet to unprecedented levels was an attempt to put a backstop in place (see **Figure 2.3**). It worked! Calm was restored, and we've had a great run in asset prices ever since. But it did *not,* however, mean that we would return to business as usual. As McCulley noted in the quote above, this crisis was not due to a lack of cash in the system. In a money system like ours, there can never be a lack of cash because cash can be "printed" at will. And the Fed did quite a bit of that, as **Figure 2.4** makes abundantly clear. The adjusted monetary base, the foundation on which the money supply is built, was more than doubled by Fed Chairman Ben Bernanke's aggressive open-market operations and continued to soar through three rounds of quantitative easing.

To create "new" money, the Fed buys existing bonds from their owners for cash. This monetizing of the debt is the modern equivalent of "priming the printing presses." One might have expected hyperinflation to result from such a surge, but instead prices fell. I'll get into the mechanics of why this happened in the following chapters. For now, suffice it to say that there was no inflation because the new money never actually entered the financial system. The banks were too scared to lend it out, and few consumers or businesses were interested in borrowing.

What I'm about to say may sound a little gloomy at first, but hear me out. I believe that we are in the early stages of a Japanese "Lost Decades" scenario, in which the pace of economic activity slows down. To be clear, I said "slows down" and not "grinds to a halt." Our economy is growing, and I expect that to continue. But I don't expect it to grow at the high rates we got used to before the crisis. We're in a different world now. Low interest rates do not have the stimulative effect they used to. Monetary policy juices the stock and bond markets but fails to work its magic on the real economy and becomes analogous to "pushing on a string." Fiscal policy (a.k.a.

taxing and spending) fails to spur the economy as well. Consumers become more conservative: They spend less on virtually everything and save more. They are less interested in borrowing from banks and less interested in loaning or investing their money in the form of speculative bonds and stocks. Banks and other investors are generally not in a position to be as generous in making loans because their balance sheets are still in need of repair after the excesses of the boom.

In any event, the end result will be a long-term slowing, in which there is less overall economic activity. Welcome to Japan, circa 1990.

I'll write at length about Japan and its economic malaise of the past two decades in a later chapter. But first, I want to make my case for why it is deflation—not inflation—that I see in the immediate future, and I will tell you what this means for your life and your investment.

CHAPTER 3:

IT'S ALL ABOUT SPENDING...OR IS IT?

Should the government "do something" to keep the economy humming along?

In fact, the government has already "done" quite a bit, running record budget deficits in recent years in its efforts to stimulate the economy. This deficit spending and the Fed's massive expansion of the monetary base have helped to keep a rough situation from getting worse. But the truth is, the government *can't* fix the biggest problem we face. It's not big or powerful enough to do so, and frankly, we wouldn't *want* it to be.

To get an idea of what I'm talking about, take a look at **Figure 3.1**. Government spending—and this includes federal, state, and local governments—accounts for only 18.2% of the economy, as measured by gross domestic product (GDP). Gross private domestic investments—which includes everything from business software expenses to the houses we live in—chips in another 16.5%. Net exports, which is negative because we have a trade deficit, contributes -2.3%.

Consumer spending, at 68.2%, completely dominates the economy. It is not Fed Chair Janet Yellen who controls the economy but Homer Simpson. Yes, Ms. Yellen probably has more power over the economy than any other single person with the power of Federal Reserve monetary policy at her disposal. But collectively, it is the Homer and Marge Simpsons of the world that make the modern consumer-based economy go. This is an important point to remember and one that I will return to shortly.

Remember the days…

Over the past decade, I've watched the media make a transformation. The 1990s were the decade of the "Money Honey," as CNBC correspondent Maria Bartiromo was known by her mostly male viewers in the investment world. I was on her show many times, much to the delight of my friends and clients. In the sunny optimism of that decade, it was only appropriate to have an attractive, smiling young woman delivering the news.

But in today's media, we have a very different ambiance. Ms. Bartiromo is still around, but her style is markedly different. The smile has been replaced by cynicism. And perhaps most tellingly, Ms. Bartiromo herself is less of a media figure than she used to be. Today, reflecting the mood of the times, the news is more often delivered by the somber, scowling likes of Glenn Beck.

I mention Glenn Beck because I have heard him say, with righteous indignation, that "runaway" consumer spending was bankrupting the country. But is this statement remotely accurate? Has America really become a country of degenerate spendthrifts? Looking at **Figure 3.1**, I can understand why you might say yes. But the historical facts do not support this view at all.

Take a look at **Figure 3.2**, which tracks the components of **Figure 6.1** historically. As you can see from even a quick look, consumer spending was often much higher than 70% in past decades. It fell to less than half of GDP during World War II, which is understandable. The entire American economy was on war footing at the time, and a large percentage of male would-be consumers were driving tanks in Europe and Asia. After the war, government spending and investment both remained higher than in past decades. Again, this stands to reason. The modern welfare state, for better or worse, was born in the 1930s and came of age in the 1940s and 1950s. Investment spending was also turbocharged by the building of America's suburbs as the GIs came home and started large families in what we now call the Baby Boom. This was also the period that saw the construction of America's largest and most significant public works project in history: the Interstate Highway System.

Figure 3.1: Who Spends What in the Economy 2014

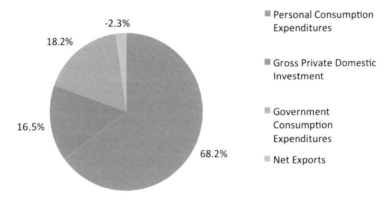

Source: U.S. Bureau of Economic Analysis

Figure 3.2: Composition of U.S. Gross Domestic Product

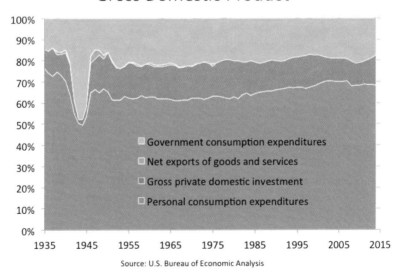

Source: U.S. Bureau of Economic Analysis

The recent surge in government spending notwithstanding, government expenditures and investment spending have been in decline, falling as a percentage of GDP, and consumer spending has grown to fill the void. Why anyone would consider this bad news is beyond me. This is great news. Adam Smith, the father of economics, said so himself in *The Wealth of Nations: "Consumption is the sole end and purpose of all production."*

Unfortunately, this means that stimulus spending from Washington is unlikely to have much of an effect other than to stretch an already busted budget. Similar programs didn't work in Japan, and there is no reason to believe they will work here. I do understand there are massive differences between the United States and Japan. The most important is that the Japanese do not have a sizable generation waiting in the wings to make up for the aging Baby Boomer generation, while the United States does in the Echo Boomers (also called the Millennials and Generation Y), which are the kids of the Baby Boomers. However, those kids are still several years away from being able to spend at the level of their parents.

No, it's *not* different this time. In a modern consumer economy, stimulus spending doesn't work because it *can't*. Period.

It's All About Consumer Spending.

So, we've established that consumer spending is the 800-pound gorilla in the U.S. economy. As goes the consumer, so goes the economy.

The good news is that this makes the economy highly predictable. The bad news is that demographic trends suggest the American consumer may be in for several years of sluggish spending.

You have heard me mention Harry Dent before, and in this section I want to explain his demographic research and its implications for the consumer and, by proxy, the economy. Harry Dent brought to the world of financial and investment research the insights that marketers have used since the dawn of capitalism: **Consumer spending decisions are driven largely**

Figure 3.3: Spending By Stage of Life

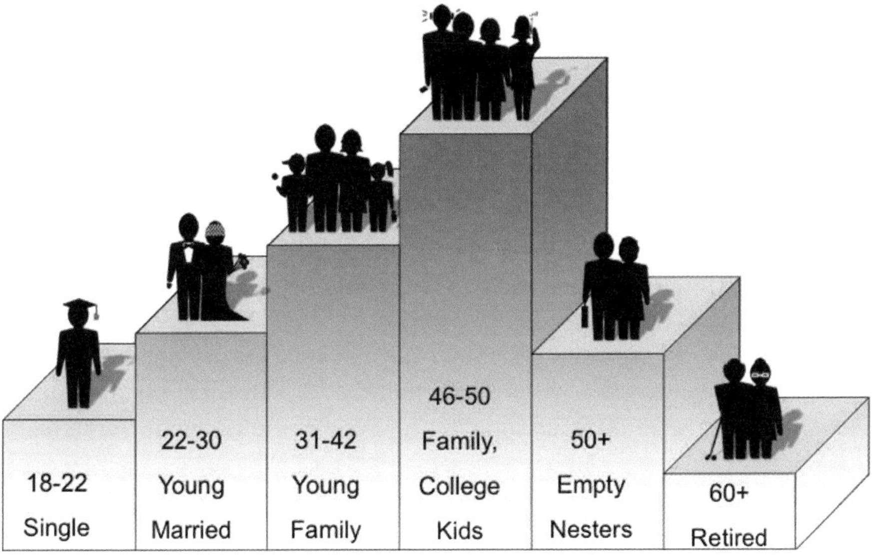

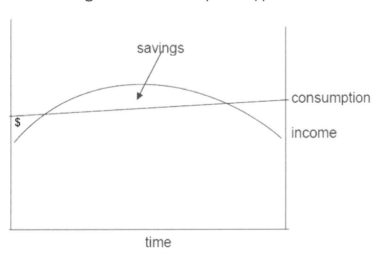

Source: HS Dent Foundation (HSDent.com)

Figure 3.4: Life Cycle Hypothesis

savings

consumption

income

$

time

Source: Stevens, 2004

by age and stage of life. (see Figure 3.3).

Academic economists have touched on this theme to an extent. Like many things in modern economics, it started with John Maynard Keynes. Lord Keynes gets a bad rap today, and, to be fair, much of it is deserved. Virtually every government in the world has rather cynically used Keynes's work to justify irresponsible deficit spending in the name of "economic stimulus." Somehow, they never seem to get to the part of Keynes's work that talks about running budget surpluses when the economy is booming in order to pay down the debts incurred from deficit spending when times were hard. Funny how that works. But while these aspects of Keynes's work tend to generate a lot of controversy, much of his lesser-known work is quite insightful. Keynes was a bright guy, even if the views for which he is most famous have been soundly discredited in the decades since his passing.

Prior to Keynes, most economic theory was focused on production, or the supply side of the equation. Consumption, driven by end-user demand, was merely an afterthought, something that just "happened" and didn't need to be explained. This was best summarized by Say's Law,[13] a maxim memorized by every freshman economics student: **"Supply creates its own demand."**

During the pits of the Great Depression, Keynes asked what should have been an obvious question: What if it *doesn't?* What if demand doesn't just "happen" as a result of the production process? What if workers opt to save their paychecks rather than spend them? What if the system, as we have grown accustomed to it, breaks down?

To answer these questions, Keynes built a simple model to explain consumer behavior (allow me to be technical here for just a minute):

$C = c_0 + c_1 Y^d$

c_0 = baseline consumption on necessities; what we must spend to survive.

c_1 = marginal propensity to consume, or the percentage of your income that you chose to spend

Y^d = income

In plain English, this means that our total spending (C) is equal to our spending on necessities (c_0) plus the percentage of our incomes that we spend on non-essentials ($c_1 Y^d$). Easy enough.

Unfortunately, this model is a little too simple. Keynes failed to note that spending and saving habits are affected by level of wealth or by age and stage of life. The same person will have a very different "marginal propensity to consume" at different points in his or her life. When we are in our early 40s, for example, we generally spend quite a bit more freely than we do at 70, when we are presumably retired and living off of our investments!

Keynes deserves credit for being the first person to approach consumption scientifically, but it is obvious that his model was incomplete and not reflective of the real world. Many of these deficiencies were addressed by the economists Modigliani, Brumberg and Ando in the 1950s and 60s in what became known as the Life Cycle Hypothesis (**Figure 3.4**).

These economists graphically displayed what every household intuitively knows. People follow a life cycle of earning and spending. In the early stages of our careers, our incomes are low relative to our expenses, often forcing us to take out large debts for homes, cars, appliances, etc. In middle age, we earn enough money to meet all of our current expenses, plus save for retirement. And naturally in retirement, our income falls and we slowly spend down our savings. Makes sense.

This model, though more advanced than Keynes', is still problematic. Notice that income makes a curve while consumption makes a straight line. This chart is suggesting that our consumer spending increases in a mild, linear fashion from birth until death. I'll get into why that's not an accurate representation shortly.

In 1957, the great economist Milton Friedman made his own modifications to the Consumption Function and to the Life Cycle Hypothesis and dubbed it the "Permanent Income Hypothesis." Friedman's idea was this: People base their consumer spending on what they consider their "permanent" income, or their average income over time. They do this in an attempt to maintain a relatively constant standard of living, even though their incomes may vary wildly over time and particularly as they age. We don't shop at Saks Fifth Avenue one day and then at Goodwill the next because we had a single bad pay period. Our lifestyle remains more or less constant, even as income fluctuates.

This goes a long way in explaining why Americans love consumer debt as much as they do. It's ok to spend more than you make today, because your salary will be high enough after that next promotion to pay it all back.

Keynes's model, remember, assumed that people spend a constant proportion of their current incomes. Friedman assumes that people are forward-looking and base consumption decisions today on income expectations for tomorrow. Changes in current income, if perceived to be temporary, have little effect on spending. Friedman correctly realized that a family's standard of living is "sticky." When Dad's bonus check is a little disappointing one year, the family does not instantly eschew Cadillac in favor of Chevrolet. Whether for pride, concern for their children, or simple inertia, Americans are slow to ratchet down their lifestyles.

Friedman's model, though interesting, is also deeply flawed. Like the Life Cycle models, it assumes that spending rises indefinitely into the future. Intuitively, we all know this isn't true. As we age, we become far more conservative in our spending habits. This is partially out of economic necessity, in that most Americans live on a fixed income in retirement from Social Security, annuities, bonds, or pension payments, and their budget must fit within those means. But perhaps even more important than this natural conservatism that comes with age is the fact that, at some point, we have already made all of life's major purchases. We tend to drive less as we age, meaning that we replace our cars less often. We already own the largest and most expensive home we are likely to ever

Figure 3.5: Household Spending By Age

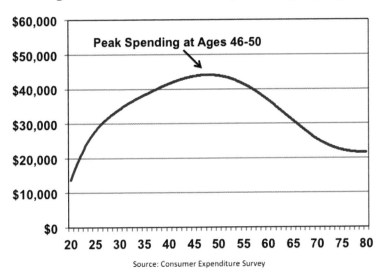

Source: Consumer Expenditure Survey

Figure 3.6: HS Dent Modified Life Cycle Hypothesis

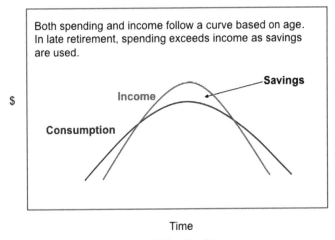

Source: HS Dent Foundation

live in, and we have already stuffed it full of furniture and appliances. Apart from basic necessities and leisure activities, there is simply not that much to spend our money on!

While we know all of this intuitively, it is nice to be able to back it up with hard statistics. Using data from the U.S. Consumer Expenditure Survey, we see that consumer spending is largely a function of age (**Figure 3.5**). We spend increasingly more raising our families until our late 40s or early 50s, after which time we pare down our spending and save for retirement. Consider **Figure 3.6**. In this case, the income line has the same basic shape as in **Figure 3.4**, though the consumption line has been transformed into a curve, like **Figure 3.5** would suggest.

With this insight, I'd like to get into the meat of this research. What is true of the individual is also true of the country as a whole. Entire generations follow this HS Dent Modified Life Cycle, accumulating debts to buy cars, homes and perhaps education for their children, and then paying off these debts to save for retirement. The Baby Boomers—the biggest and richest generation in history—are now entering the tail end of this cycle. The Boomers are now at a stage of their lives where it no longer makes sense to take on new debts. They are deleveraging, paying off their debts, for two critical reasons:

1. It is a natural cycle.

2. Because they have to!

An over-indebted, over-leveraged population always occurs at the bottom of economic cycles, but not typically as bad as this one. As an example of excess, never before have people without money or a source of income been able to borrow to buy a home in which there is no possible way for them to pay it back. This is a big reason why I see deflation persisting for much longer than most economists think.

Do you think this sounds too simplistic? I can assure you that, yes, it really is that simple. I'll start from the basics and build my case. The demographic argument is compelling, and most of my clients instinctively

Figure 3.7: Immigration Adjusted Birth Index

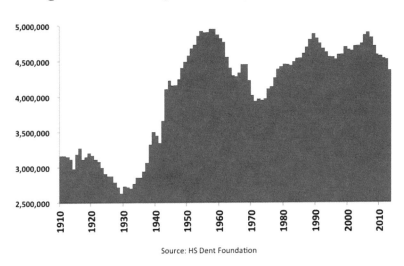

Source: HS Dent Foundation

Figure 3.8: Immigration Adjusted Birth Index

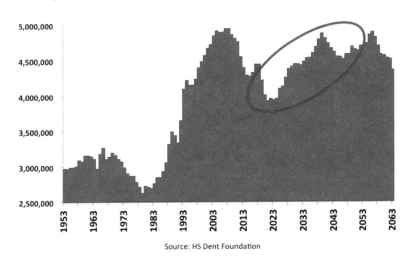

Source: HS Dent Foundation

get it when I explain it to them. Armed with this information, I wrote my special report: An Economic Tsunami Lies Ahead – How to Prepare for This Perfect Storm (see Appendix A), which forecasted and predicted the current economic malaise we are currently in and subsequent stock market crash.

Let's start at the beginning—with births. The U.S. National Center for Health Statistics tracks the number of babies born every year. To account for immigrants who were not born here, we add the number of immigrants by their birth year to the U.S. numbers. This gives us the Immigration-Adjusted Birth Index (**Figure 3.7**), which was first developed by Harry Dent.

This is where the analysis gets interesting. If we know how many Americans we have by birth year and we know at what age they tend to buy something, we suddenly have a very powerful forecasting tool.

As an example, let's consider an example near and dear to parents and grandparents: college education. Take a look at **Figure 3.9**, which is a close-up of the circled area in **Figure 3.8** with an important twist. In **Figure 3.9**, we push the circled portion of **Figure 3.8** forward by 18 years to account for the age that most kids go to college.

Have you ever noticed how competitive it is to get into a good school these days? And how expensive too, for that matter? When I was looking at universities as a young man, having a decent set of high school grades and perhaps having an extracurricular activity or two was more than sufficient to get into a good school. These days, a kid has to have a 4.0+ GPA, be a concert-caliber musician, throw a football like a Heisman candidate, and spend a summer feeding homeless children in India to even be considered. After looking at **Figure 3.9**, you can see why. The huge generation that is made of up the children of the Baby Boomers—the Echo Boomers—has been busting the capacity of America's universities. The demand for college education has far outstripped supply, causing competition for admission slots and tuition expenses to soar.

Yes, it is simple economics. When demand is higher than supply,

Figure 3.9: The College Admissions Wave
Births Lagged 18 Years

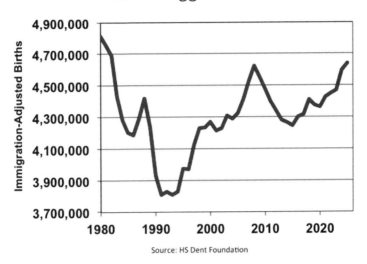

Source: HS Dent Foundation

Figure 3.10: The Spending Wave

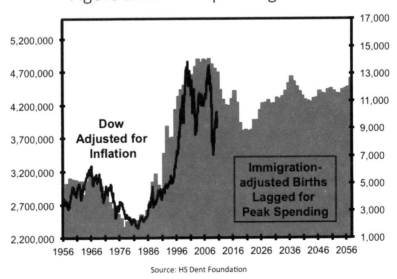

Source: HS Dent Foundation

prices rise. In the case of college admissions, the "price" is both monetary and merit-based in the form of higher test scores and admissions standards.

Getting back into consumer spending, we know that Americans tend to peak in their consumer spending at around age 48. Applying this insight to the same methodology we used above, we get one of the most powerful predictors ever invented, the *Spending Wave* (**Figure 3.10**), also developed by Harry Dent.

The Spending Wave is one of the most useful tools in demographic research. As you can see, the Dow Jones Industrial Average adjusted for inflation had a strong resemblance to the Immigration-Adjusted Birth Index. When you lag the Birth Index by 48 years to account for the average age of peak spending, the two charts move together uncannily.

Again, intuitively, this makes a lot of sense. As I mentioned above, it is the Homer and Marge Simpsons that drive nearly 70% of the U.S. economy. Over the long-term, the stock market's movement is a reflection of economic growth. So, over very long-term periods, demographic trends should have a significant impact on stock prices.

Demographic trends most certainly do *not* determine what the day-to-day fluctuations of the market will be. In the short-term, "noise" factors and current events have a far greater impact. Demographic trends do not necessarily pinpoint market meltdowns, such as the one in late 2008 that was ignited by the Lehman Brothers failure.

As the market has become more volatile in recent years, the neat, clean correlation on the Spending Wave has become a little more jagged. The point of the chart, however, is still very obvious: Demographic trends suggest that stock returns will be pretty choppy in the years ahead. The Dow may or may not continue the downward track projected by the Spending Wave; only time will tell. But suffice it to say, the fantastic returns that we all got used to in the 1980s and 1990s—and particularly from 2009-2014—are likely a thing of the past for at least the foreseeable future,

Hey, it is certainly possible that, despite the negative demographic trends and the continued menace of debt deflation, stocks could enjoy positive returns in the years ahead. But given the risks, this is clearly not a time to throw caution to the wind with *your* hard-earned retirement dollars.

Attention, Demographics and the Stock Market

In 2005, Stefano DellaVigna and Joshua Pollet published one of the most insightful papers in the history of academic finance: "Attention, Demographics, and the Stock Market." DellaVigna and Pollet wrote,

> *We consider the case of demographic information. Cohort size fluctuations produce forecastable demand changes for age-sensitive sectors, such as toys, bicycles, beer, life insurance, and nursing homes. These demand changes are predictable once a specific cohort is born.*

What the professors are saying is that demographic information can be used to predict the demand for certain products. Consider college dorm rooms. Allowing for changes in the percentage of kids attending college, school administrators can budget their need for dorm rooms 18 years in advance. A surge in births today means a surge in demand for dorm beds 18 years from now, and a slowdown in births today means a slowdown in demand for dorm beds. This same logic can be applied to stock market sectors as well. As the professors continue,

> *We use lagged consumption and demographic data to forecast future consumption demand growth induced by changes in age structure. We find that demand forecasts predict profitability by industry. Moreover, forecasted demand changes 5 to 10 years in the future predict annual industry stock returns.* ***One additional percentage point of annualized demand growth due to demographics predicts a 5 to 10 percentage point increase in annual abnormal industry stock returns.*** *However, forecasted demand changes over shorter horizons do not predict stock returns.*

This last point—that demographic analysis works better over longer time horizons—makes a lot of sense when you consider that the average holding period for stocks is less than a year. Investors, both professional and amateur, are known to be "myopic" in their behavior. They look at quarterly earnings per share growth, or if they are technicians, they look at what the stock price is doing *today*. Demographic trends are slow moving and, frankly, boring. The frenetic bustle you see on CNBC is *sexy*. But demographics? Yeah, not so much.

But herein lies our opportunity. If we have the patience to assemble a solid portfolio of strong investments supported by durable demographic trends, we can quietly post good returns without being distracted by the noise.

DellaVigna and Pollet conclude that the demographic model works better for industries with "higher barriers to entry and with more pronounced age patterns in consumption." This only stands to reason. High barriers to entry prevent new Johnny-come-lately companies from quickly jumping in to satisfy excess, demographic-driven demand. It also makes sense that it works better for products with pronounced age patterns. Demographics can tell you how much demand there will be for artificial knees or nursing homes. But they're not going to tell you a lot about demand for General Electric aircraft engines.

This brings a new element to the use of demographics as an investment tool. Not only can demographic trends be used from a "macro" perspective, but from a "micro" perspective as well to identify promising companies and sectors. Of course, these insights are not limited to passive portfolio investors. Successful entrepreneurs can and do use it every day.

Entrepreneurs often have a better idea of what's happening in the real economy than portfolio managers. It only makes sense; while a portfolio manager can easily get lost in the world of abstract financial jargon, a successful entrepreneur has to roll up his sleeves and work in the real world. As investors, we would likely be more successful in our stock picking if we approached the process with an entrepreneur's mindset.

A few years ago, I was delighted to see that the *Financial Times* reported on a pair of young entrepreneurs who have built a successful retailing business following these same principles.[15]

In 2005, Marc Lore and Vinit Bharara launched Diapers.com, an e-commerce site selling diapers and other baby products.

"We came across the baby market," the *Financial Times* quotes Mr. Lore. "It was a $40B market and incredibly fragmented online, with lots of players but no number-one brand. So we thought: 'We need to build a brand, and not do it by beating rivals on keyword marketing [to attract internet searches].'"

In its first five years of existence, Diapers.com has become a $275 million business and a top "pure play" e-commerce site not associated with a traditional retailer. The owners claim the site has become the biggest online seller of infant car seats and that it sells four times as many diapers as Amazon.com. Not a bad track record!

With the Millennials about to enter their baby-making years in the United States, Lore and Bharara are in the right place at the right time, and I expect their business to do well in the coming years. The family formation of the Echo Boomers should be a steady source of profits for companies like diapers.com for quite some time.

Of course, demographic analysis can also be used on toys of a more mature nature. Sales of large cruising motorcycles are almost entirely driven by demographic trends. And unfortunately, the news just doesn't get better for Harley-Davidson and its peers in the "big bike" business.

Harley is a true American icon. Its motorcycles are so distinctive that the company actually tried to trademark the "Harley sound," that familiar rumble of the bikes' exhaust, back in the mid-1990s.

It's also a well-managed company and one of those true rarities:

A successful turnaround story. This is a company that was facing bankruptcy in the early 1980s, yet managed to rebuild itself into the pride of American manufacturing ... and the subject of countless case studies in MBA programs worldwide.

Harley's management was able to pull off that coup by leveraging that intangible quality that is so hard to imitate: brand cachet. For a particular breed of leather-wearing motorcycle enthusiasts, there is simply nothing on par with a Harley.

Unfortunately, none of that matters. Harley's sales have been in free fall for nearly a decade now. Harley sold 349,196 bikes in 2006, and sales dropped to an estimated 270,000 bikes in 2014. That's a decline of over a quarter, and remember, the economy has been on the mend for over five years. You can't blame those numbers on a bad economy or expensive gas.

Harley's big bikes are a product purchased almost exclusively by white males in their mid-to-late 40s. All of this was well and good 10 years ago when the Baby Boomers first began to enter this demographic sweet spot. Harley never had it better. The largest generation in history had just become their best customer.

Unfortunately, those days are gone. The Boomer male has passed this stage and has likely shaved off the goatee and closeted the leather jacket. The number of American men aged 45-49 peaked in 2010 and has been in decline ever since. Demographic projections show that the number of 45- to 49-year-old men won't recover to its 2010 high until well after 2030. So, Harley is pretty well screwed here. And I say this, again, as an admirer of the company!

Try as Harley might to reach out to other demographic consumer groups—younger and non-Caucasian men and women, for example—Harley's future has already been written. Sales of the company's iconic bikes should continue to disappoint investors for the foreseeable future, barring the occasional surprise.

Harley's management isn't blind to this, by the way. They actually have a section on their website dedicated to the demographic issues the company faces! If you don't believe me, go to *http://investor. harley-davidson.com/* and click on the "Demographics" link on the menu to the left of the screen.

Across the Atlantic, changing demographics are wreaking havoc on another iconic industry—German beer.

Normally it's not considered politically correct to play on national stereotypes, but the Germans themselves have cultivated a macho image as a nation that knows how to knock back a stein or two. Visiting a proper Bavarian biergarten and ordering an obscenely large beer (from a barmaid with biceps big enough to beat most Harley bikers at arm wrestling) is practically a rite of passage for visitors to the country.

So, it might come as a surprise that German beer consumption is in a long-term decline. Figures here are a little dated, but according to the *Economist*, German beer drinking has declined from 142 liters per

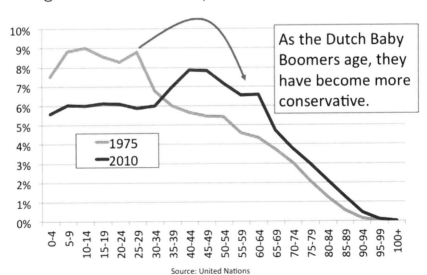

Figure 3.11: Dutch Population, 1975 vs. 2010

As the Dutch Baby Boomers age, they have become more conservative.

1975
2010

Source: United Nations

person per year in 1991 to "only" 110 liters in 2009.

That's still a lot of beer, mind you. Enough to put most Americans accustomed to watery Bud Light in the hospital. Still, that is a decline of more than a fifth.

As you might guess, demographics are the driving force behind this change. As the *Economist* explains, "An ageing, shrinking population is drinking less… Even among the traditionally hard-boozing middle-aged, health concerns have curbed drinking."It's not just German beer consumption that is suffering in Europe, however.

The Dutch are getting a little more restrictive on their cannabis cafes and red light district. It appears that the Dutch—world-famous for their socially liberal attitudes—are becoming significantly less tolerant as the years go by. As a simple measuring gauge, the number of cannabis cafes has halved since 1995, from roughly 1,400 to 700.[18]

So, what is the story? Are the Dutch tired of being known as the world's pimps and drug dealers? Has the novelty simply worn off? What is making Dutch society become more socially conservative?

One obvious answer is that the Dutch are tired of seeing American and British youths making buffoons of themselves in their smoky cafes. The liberal policies regarding drugs and prostitution tend to attract the wrong kind of tourist. But there is a larger issue at play as well, and as you might guess, demographics are at the center of it. And I'm not talking about the influx of North African Muslim immigrants, which is a major issue these days in Dutch politics. No, I'm talking about the Dutch Baby Boomers (Figure 3.11).

As you can see in the chart, the Netherlands was a young country in 1975. The Dutch Baby Boomers were teenagers and 20-somethings at that time. Not surprisingly, the cannabis cafes became legal in 1976, when the Baby Boomers as a generation were in their prime years of misspent youth.

As the Boomers in both the United States and Europe have aged, they have maintained a fair bit of the personality of their younger years, a mixture of anti-establishment rebelliousness and wide-eyed idealism.

But in other ways, they have become their parents. In fact, in some ways they are far stricter. Boomer parents were notorious about coddling their children and micromanaging every aspect of their lives. Perhaps, remembering their own wilder years, they didn't trust their kids with the same amount of freedom that they themselves enjoyed.

The Boomers have also become wealthier as they have aged, and perhaps these bourgeois bohemians consider the seedy element associated with drugs and prostitution to be bad for property values.

I could write an entire book of nothing but demographic anecdotes like these, but I will spare you for now. With an understanding of this material, there are certainly attractive investment opportunities out there, and I'll get into my recommendations in a later chapter. But first, I want to dive into demographics from a different angle.

CHAPTER 4:

PREDICTING THE STOCK MARKET THROUGH DEMOGRAPHICS

People often ask how I have gotten the economic and market cycles right. In the big picture it's not all that difficult. If you know when and how people spend their money during their life, all you need to do is figure out how many people there are in the various stages of life.

Do you think Mattel just makes Barbie dolls until too much hair gets stuck in the conveyor belt and the machine breaks or that Hasbro makes GI Joes until they get sick of his Kung Fu grip? Of course not! Mattel and Hasbro conduct intense demographic research to see how many 4–10 year old girls and 5–11 year old boys there are and will be. And believe it or not, we know precisely how people spend their money from the first allowance dollar they get from mom and dad to the day you die. Now I'm not the first person to write about the effects of an aging society on stock prices, of course. In the last chapter, I mentioned the groundbreaking work of DellaVigna, Pollet and Dent. Naturally, there are also other views, often conflicting, that I want to discuss in this chapter.

Professor Jeremy Siegel of the Wharton School of Business is one of the most respected minds in the world of investment research and for good reason. His *Stocks for the Long Run* is a solid piece of research that belongs on every investor's shelf. While Siegel can be dogmatic in his defense of equities (there seems to be no circumstance in which Siegel wouldn't recommend buying stocks), his work is top notch and should be taken seriously.

Unfortunately, I can't say the same for his demographic research. Professor Siegel, former Fed Chairman Ben Bernanke, and popular financial writer and speaker Robert Kiyosaki have all written about demographics in a similar way. For simplicity's sake, I'll lump them all together as "the Siegel view." At its roots, the Siegel view is a variation of the life cycle models I covered in the last chapter.

The San Francisco Federal Reserve Bank explored the Siegel view before Siegel himself. Cogley and Royer's 1998 paper "The Baby Boom, the Baby Bust, and Asset Markets" summarizes Siegel's basic model:

> To understand the relation between demography and capital markets, it is useful to think about the Life Cycle model of consumption and saving. Roughly speaking, the Life Cycle model states that people work and save when they are young and live off the proceeds when they retire…(See **Figure 7.1**)
>
> [They] work until age 65, at which time they begin to sell off assets and live off the proceeds. The key feature… is that wealth has a hump shape over the life cycle. It peaks at retirement age and then begins to decline. **In other words, older people tend to be net sellers of financial assets.**

In an economy with a stable age distribution, this would have no effect on capital markets. When each cohort reached retirement age, it would sell its assets to younger cohorts who were accumulating wealth, and with steady population growth there would always be enough of the latter to absorb the sales of the former. But what happens when population growth isn't steady and the economy's age distribution isn't stable? In particular, what happens when the old-age dependency ratio rises, and there are proportionally fewer young savers to buy up the assets of the older retirees? In this case, by the law of supply and demand, one would expect the price of assets to fall. As aging baby boomers begin to sell their financial assets, they will presumably be selling to the next waves of savers, the so-called Generation Xers and Yers, which are significantly smaller population cohorts. With relatively fewer buyers than in the past, boomers may find themselves selling into a weak market when they retire.[19]

The problem with this argument is that is it so close to being correct. In a free economy, prices for everything are determined by supply and demand. Even in cases where prices are fixed, such as in rent-control policies and socialized medicine, the "price" finds a way to adjust to supply and demand. In cases like these where the dollar price is not allowed to fluctuate, prices adjust through mechanisms like rationing or waiting lists—a higher "price" is a longer wait.

Naturally, stocks are no exception. In fact, the stock market is as close to a "pure" free market as has ever existed, with prices changing almost instantly to reflect every infinitesimal shift in sentiment by traders. *Forbes* columnist Ken Fisher explores this idea in his delightfully irreverent book *The Only Three Things That Count*: "There are just two factors in this whole, wide, wonderful and whacky world driving stock prices. Always and everywhere, stock prices are derived singularly by shifts in supply and demand…These dueling pressures in supply and demand set prices of all we buy."

So, demand constantly shifts with the whims and emotions of traders, but what about the *supply* of stock? At any given time, the float of traded shares is relatively fixed. Sure, Bill Gates could massively increase the supply of Microsoft by dumping his personal holdings, but significant insider sales tend to be rare. And in this case, we are talking about *existing* shares being floated. What about new shares? What about entirely new companies going public?

"Shifts in supply are different," Fisher continues. "In the short run, the actual supply of securities is almost completely fixed, as it takes time and effort and a cooperative multiplicity of players to create new shares or destroy existing ones. Think about how long IPOs or mergers need to evolve, and the amount of advance notice the companies are required by law to give the public."

Adding new supply is expensive, time-consuming, and depends on a lot of complex factors. As Fisher continues, "…no matter what anyone would have you believe, no one has any way to predict supply in the far distant future. This is among the reasons why long-term mechanical forecasting notions are usually way, way wide of the mark. No one knows what whacky things may happen to the creation or destruction of the supply of equities 5 to 20 years from now."

This is the flaw in the "supply side" of the Siegel demographic argument. In this modified Life Cycle theory, stock trading takes place within a closed "box." There is no consideration for new issues of stock, executive stock options, share buybacks, or even mergers and bankruptcies.

There are failings in the demand side as well. This modified Life Cycle hypothesis assumes that rank and file Americans uniformly accumulate stocks throughout their working lives and then slowly sell them off in retirement. As Cogley and Royer discuss above, this is problematic because the large Boomer generation has no one to sell its holdings to.

As intuitive—and scary—as this explanation sounds, it doesn't hold up to a critical analysis. First, it rather "democratically" assumes that ownership of stock is dominated by rank-and-file Americans through their IRAs, 401ks and brokerage accounts. As an egalitarian society, this is how we prefer to view the world. Unfortunately, it is patently false. The stock market is not a one-man-one-vote democracy in which the little guy makes a difference; it is a plutocracy in which the "big money" dominates. Consider **Figure 7.2**. After decades of growing participation through vehicles such as retirement accounts, mutual funds and discounted brokerage accounts, more than half of Americans still hold no stock in any form. Even more telling, *only about 30% of households have stock holdings of over $10,000*. And remember, these numbers only go through the mid-2000s, which is as recent as reliable data was available. After the market meltdown of 2008, it is safe to assume the percentages are now lower.

But what about those Boomers who *do* own stocks? Even if a majority of Americans own no stock, might the selling by a large minority be significant enough to chop the market down a few notches? And wouldn't demographic trends suggest that this was likely?

Again, this explanation doesn't hold up to critical analysis. While **Figure 7.2** indicates how many Americans own stocks, **Figure 7.3** takes a closer look at those who do. It is immediately obvious that the overwhelming majority of stock market wealth is controlled by a small percentage of Americans. The top 10% wealthiest own a full 81% of the stock market. The top 1% alone controls 35%! Meanwhile, 80% of the population (the 401ks and IRAs) holds just 8% of the total.

The typical upper-middle-class Baby Boomer with a 401k balance of a couple hundred thousand dollars or even a million or two will most likely be selling stocks in his golden years to fund his living expenses. He will gradually shift mostly out of stocks and into income investments like bonds. Chances are good that the income alone won't be sufficient, so he will slowly spend down his principal as well. Or, he may opt to sell all of his stocks and bonds at once and buy an annuity. This is standard financial planning, and it is exactly what he should do. But as **Figure 7.3** demonstrates, this periodic retirement selling is like a drop in the ocean. Bill Gates and Warren Buffett won't be selling their stock holdings to fund retirement, and neither will the rest of the top 10% of stockholders that control 81% of the market. It is the middle class—the 80% of the population that owns less than 10% of the equity—that follows the Life Cycle Hypothesis, not the rich.

Even though the *stock market* is still dominated by the rich, the American economy is dominated by the middle class, the "mass affluent." A good way to illustrate this is to look at wealth tied to home ownership. As seen in **Figure 7.4**, the top 5% still owns a disproportionate share of the country's real estate. But the key here is that it is the bottom 80% that dominates, not the top tier.

The same holds true for the overall economy. It is the middle class that fills the aisles of Best Buy, Wal-Mart and the Home Depot. It is the discretionary income of mainstream Americans that allow new Starbucks franchises to sprout up like weeds. And it is, ultimately, this same middle-class America that should cause stock market gains to be somewhat tepid going forward, but not for the same reasons that Jeremy Siegel and his contemporaries believe.

I said it before, and I'll say it again: Consumer spending drives economic growth. In the end, it's the only real reason we go to work in the morning. As the rank-and-file of the Baby Boomer generation passes its peak spending years, it will begin to curtail its spending and increase its savings. Less consumption means less need for production and retail. This means factory orders slow down. Fewer big-box stores get built. Fewer trucks are needed to transport fewer goods to fewer stores. This effect ripples throughout the economy— there is demand for fewer truck stops selling fewer energy drinks, packs of gum and embroidered trucker caps.

The Boomers' consumer spending has been the engine that makes this entire machine move. A decline in spending growth has a ripple effect that should lead to a slowdown in corporate profits—and ultimately a slower rate of return for stock prices. Thus, demographics can be used as a highly effective forecasting tool, but doing so requires that you "connect the dots." The problem with the academic models used by Siegel and the Fed is that they are too simple. Supply and demand drive the market, but they ultimately do so based on investor expectations of future earnings. And demographics are the best long-term indicator for the direction of future earnings. This was the insight of DellaVigna and Pollet's research on individual stocks, and in my view, the correct way to understand the effect of demographics on stock prices.

Speaking of prices, I'm dedicating one last chapter to demographics. I will explore how people, not just monetary policy, affect the rate of inflation.

CHAPTER 5:

INFLATION OR DEFLATION WAVE AHEAD? THE ANSWER MAY SURPRISE YOU

You're probably thinking to yourself that with all this government stimulus and printing of dollars we have had for the last seven or eight years, we just have to have inflation, right? On the surface it makes sense. However, when you consider that massive amount of wealth that was destroyed during the last credit crises, it's easy to understand that government's enormous stimulus programs barely made a dent in what was lost.

 If you listen to the government or the Fed, you'd think that deflation is second only to the rise of Satan and slightly ahead of the bubonic plague. Here's a little factoid you might like to know before we move on. Although some would think that the Federal Reserve is part of the U.S. Government, that is not exactly the case. The Federal Reserve is actually an independent central bank whose policies do not have to be approved by the president, legislative or executive branches of government, and it does not rely on government funding.

So what's all the fuss if things cost less? Naturally, we all would like to pay less for the things we buy. So, wouldn't a period of deflation, in which the price of virtually everything falls, be good for consumers?

As it turns out, there is both good deflation and bad deflation. When a breakthrough in technology lowers the price of inputs, the producer can sell the finished good to the consumer at a lower price and still make a reasonable profit. For example, if Apple discovers a way to make its mobile processor chips cheaper, they can pass on the savings to the consumer in the form of a cheaper and more powerful iPhone. You may have heard of "Moore's Law," named after Gordon Moore, co-founder of Intel. Moore's Law states that computing power

Figure 5.1: An Economy at Equilibrium

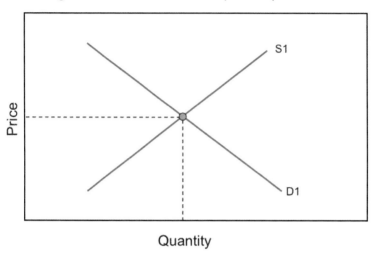

Quantity

Figure 5.2: Supply-Based "Good" Deflation

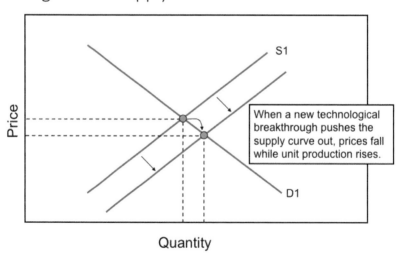

When a new technological breakthrough pushes the supply curve out, prices fall while unit production rises.

Quantity

roughly doubles every two years. Meanwhile, prices on computers continue to fall. More computational power for less money is a win for everyone. That's good deflation.

The rise of fracking lowers the cost of crude oil and, ultimately, retail gasoline. Again, everyone benefits.

Unfortunately, we also have "bad deflation," which is created from a contraction in demand, not a surge in supply.

Now, I'm going to get a little technical here, but there's no better way to say it. Consider **Figure 5.1**. S1 is the supply curve, which represents the volume of output that producers are willing and able to produce at each price. The line has a positive slope, which makes sense. Apple has a greater incentive to crank out a higher volume of iPhones when the price is higher rather than lower.

The consumer has the exact opposite motivations, as illustrated by D1, the demand curve. At lower prices, consumers are willing to buy more. In a given family budget, there might be enough cash for one

Figure 5.3: Demand-Based "Bad" Deflation

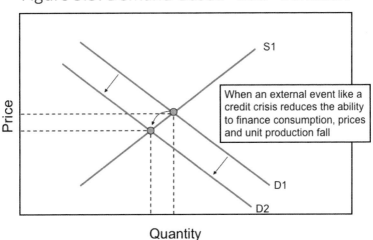

When an external event like a credit crisis reduces the ability to finance consumption, prices and unit production fall

$70 Polo shirt. But if Polo lowered the price to $10, the family has enough cash in the budget for seven shirts. Along the same lines, you might be more tempted to buy an extra Big Mac at McDonald's when they run a 99-cent special than when then charge full price. The key here is that, in general, a *decrease* in the price means an *increase* in the volume sold, and vice versa.

The point at which supply and demand intersect is the equilibrium price, the "normal" price that satisfies both the buyer and the seller. Any deviation from this equilibrium price will result in short-term shortages or surpluses. Those $10 Polo shirts are not likely to stay on the racks very long, and 99-cent Big Macs are likely to be eaten quickly—creating shortages. But that same shirt at $150 is likely to stay on the rack a lot longer, and a Big Mac priced at $10 is likely to stay under the heat lamp—creating surpluses.

Now, let us consider a situation whereby a new technological breakthrough massively reduces the cost of production, enabling companies to increase their output while simultaneously lowering their prices. This is illustrated by **Figure 5.2**, Supply-Based "Good Deflation."

As S1 is pushed out to S2, the price falls and the output rises. This has been the general trend for manufactured products since the dawn of the Industrial Revolution, and the result has been an incredible increase in real incomes and a massive improvement in the standard of living for the human race. The computer that is being used to write this book is exponentially more powerful than the ones used just 10 years ago, and it costs a fraction of the price. Computers purchased a few years from today will no doubt be exponentially more powerful than this one, and—again—a fraction of the price. This is the deflation of technological progress and productivity, and it is certainly nothing to worry about over the long term.

Technological improvements do wreak havoc on existing producers, of course. For example, the advent of mobile phones and Internet telephone providers, like Vonage and Skype, flooded the market with cheap communication tools, which caused prices to plummet. This has rendered the legacy operations of phone companies like

Verizon obsolete, and the fixed line business is quickly dying as a result. However, the benefits to society of lower communication costs far outweigh any negatives from the decline of the traditional phone companies. The increases in communication and productivity are major net positives.

In **Figure 5.3**, however, we see plenty to worry about. It shows what is happening today in the housing market and in the retail economy. Supply remains steady but the demand curve is pushed back. The result is both a lower price and lower quantity. No one wins here.

This is the key difference between good and bad deflation. In good deflation, demand remains strong and unit output increases, sometimes substantially. Profits thus can grow and companies can expand and hire new workers even as prices fall. In bad deflation, output falls and companies often are forced to shut stores or factories and to lay off workers. The auto industry is a case in point here. Facing relentless competition from stronger foreign rivals, the Big Three found themselves with a hopeless amount of excess capacity. When demand began to fall in late 2008 due to rising fuel costs and a dysfunctional credit system, they had to slash prices and offer incentives, and they still had trouble moving the metal. Before the dust settled, both General Motors and Chrysler were bankrupt and Ford just barely escaped the same fate.

What Happened?

In the case of good deflation, we know that technology and productivity are the causes. But in the current crisis, what is driving the deflationary forces? Why has the demand curve been pulled back?

The answer is simple. There are two primary components to consumer behavior: The *willingness* to spend and the *ability* to spend. Demographics are perhaps the largest contributing factor in the willingness and desire to consume, and this is a topic I'll return to in a later chapter. For now, just remember that demographic factors like age and stage of life are the primary motivators in most consumer spending decisions.

Of course, in order to actually make purchases, a consumer must have cash. Or credit.

During the recession of the early 2000s following the tech bust, free-flowing credit allowed consumers to continue spending. Strong demographic trends ensured they did exactly that. The result was a relatively mild and short-lived downturn.

This time around, the situation was fundamentally different. The collapse of the financial sector had the effect of pulling the rug out from under both the consumer and business sectors. Suddenly, consumers found themselves unable to refinance their homes to "extract equity." The home refinancing boom of the mid-2000s was a significant provider of consumer spending power that has now been effectively shut down. What bank would be reckless enough to refinance a mortgage that is now under water due to the decline in home prices?

Five years into a recovery, Americans are spending money again, though the mindset is still very different. Shoppers are more careful with their cash these days, preferring to wait for sales and look for bargains. And the rough patch following the meltdown really accelerated trends that were already in play, such as the movement of retail from physical stores to the Internet. Smartphones have enabled shoppers to be even savvier, allowing them to compare prices in real time.

Do you have any relatives—perhaps a grandparent or aunt—who lived through the Great Depression? Though there aren't too many of that great generation left, most of us can fondly remember a loved one that lived through that hard period. And most of us will chuckle to ourselves remembering how frugal they were. The Depression shaped their financial habits for the rest of their lives.

Well, guess what? The Millennials have a lot of the same personality characteristics. The Boomers and Generation X both grew up in an

Figure 5.4: Capacity Utilization

Source: Federal Reserve

Figure 5.5: Demand-Based Inflation

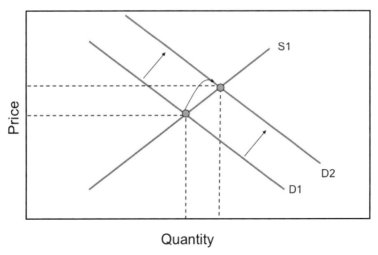

era of abundance and of booming stock markets. The Millennials were kids during the great technology bust of 2000-2002 and young adults during the 2008 financial meltdown. As young people, the Millennials don't get a lot of respect. But they are probably the most financially responsible generation America has seen in 70 years.

Want an example? Millennials watch TV like the rest of us. But they don't pay for it. Inflation in cable TV prices has massively outpaced broad-based consumer price inflation, and Millennials have responded by "cutting the cord" and watching their favorite shows on their laptops, iPads or via Netflix.

Want hard numbers? A recent poll found that one in four Millennials have cut the cord or have never paid for cable, though a majority had paid for cheaper online services such as Netflix, Amazon Instant Video or Hulu Plus. HBO saw the handwriting on the wall here and announced plans to sell its content as a cheaper, stand-alone streaming service rather than exclusively via an expensive cable subscription.

Figure 5.6: U.S. Federal Budget Surplus and Deficit in $Billions

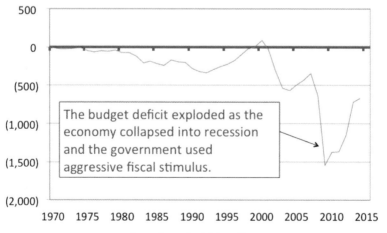

Source: Congressional Budget Office

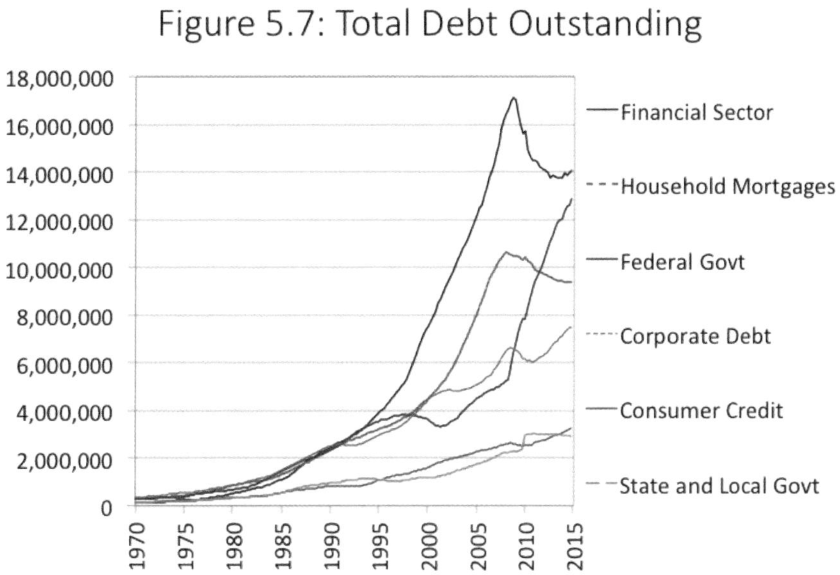

Figure 5.7: Total Debt Outstanding

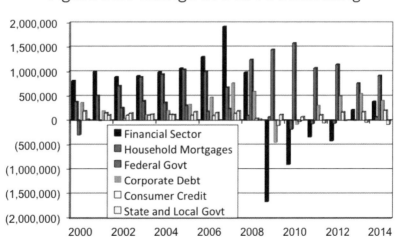

Source: Federal Reserve Flow of Funds Report (FRB Z1)

Figure 5.8: Change in Debt Outstanding

Source: Federal Reserve Flow of Funds Report (FRB Z1)

Millennials, more than any generation in recent memory, are also a lot more likely to live with their parents. The most recent statistics show 36% of 18- to 31-year-olds currently live with their parents.

Now, I'm not criticizing the Millennials here. In fact, I respect their fiscal discipline. But this is a generation that is not accustomed to spending money like the Baby Boomers and Gen X. Though they may have very different tastes in clothes and music, this generation has a lot more in common with the pre-World War II Depression era generation.

Why Is This a Problem?

The psychological aspect is perhaps the scariest part. The fear of deflation can become a self-fulfilling prophecy, and when it does, economic activity grinds to a halt. As unpleasant as inflation is, it is the fear of deflation that keeps Fed chairmen awake at night. Before taking the job, Ben Bernanke was known infamously as "Helicopter Ben" for comments made about deflation. To paraphrase, Mr. Bernanke said, only half joking, that the Federal Reserve would do anything in its power to avoid deflation, even if it meant literally dumping dollars out of helicopters in the hopes that someone would spend them. (Current Fed Chair Janet Yellen has made similar comments over the years.)

It is also worth mentioning that when Franklin Delano Roosevelt famously said "The only thing we have to fear is fear itself," he referred not to the Nazi regime or of looming war. No, Roosevelt meant the vicious cycle of pessimism brought on by deflation, which he went on to call a "nameless, unreasoning, unjustified terror which paralyzes needed efforts to convert retreat into advance."

What Now?

With demand being slack these last several years, there has been very little new investment in property, plant and equipment outside of, say, the energy sector. Instead of pouring money into their businesses, corporate managements have used their excess cash to boost dividends and buy

Figure 5.9: Money Supply M3

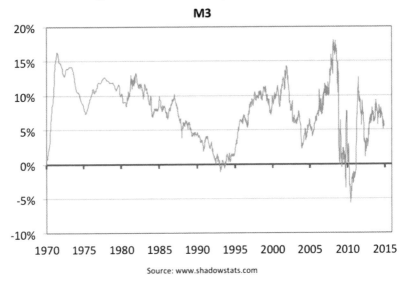

Source: www.shadowstats.com

Figure 5.10: Velocity of Money
GDP to M2 Money Supply

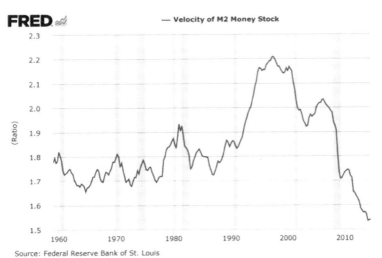

Source: Federal Reserve Bank of St. Louis

Shaded areas indicate US recessions - 2014 research.stlouisfed.org

back shares. That's not a bad thing, mind you, and it's actually worked out quite well for investors over the past six years. The shrinking float of available shares due to buybacks has boosted earnings per share and given the bull market the equivalent of a turbo charge. Only now, six years into economic recovery, has the excess capacity been mopped up (**Figure 5.4**). Capacity utilization measures what percentage of our production capacity is currently being used. As you can see, it had rebounded from the pits of late 2009, but even after the recovery it is barely higher that it was during the *lows* of the early 1900s recession. That tells me that there's still not a lot of pricing power out there. In most areas of consumer spending, it's still a buyer's market.

Demographic trends suggest that these conditions can linger far longer than most economists think. As the Baby Boomers accelerate the downsizing of their lives in preparation for retirement, aggregate demand will be sorely lacking in the economy. These conditions still linger in Japan, nearly 20 years after the Japanese stock and property bubbles reached their explosive peaks and collapsed.

President Obama, like former President Bush, understands the dangers of deflation and throughout his presidency has tried to "legislate" inflation through federal fiscal stimulus. As illustrated in **Figure 5.5**, the president has used deficit spending to try to push the demand curve forward, thus raising prices. It's debatable whether it has worked. And even if you argue it has "worked," it's really just masked the problem rather than fixed the inherent condition, creating yet another bubble in government debt. This will produce an effect similar to that of Viagra, temporary but good while it lasts. I suppose you can't blame the president for trying, but once the history books are written, the stimulus plans of the 2010s will not be any more effective than those undertaken in Japan during the 1990s. More on that to come.

Are the Government's Actions Inflationary?

If you are reading this book, chances are good that you have a stake in the system. You likely either have a successful career or are retired after a lifetime of hard work. You pay your taxes, you vote, and if you are like me, you are concerned about the ballooning federal budget deficit (**Figure 5.6**). As individuals, we would never consistently spend more money than we make. To do so would be irresponsible. Yet this is exactly what our government does year after year, regardless of which party is in power.

In its efforts to stimulate the economy, the government has run previously unimaginable budget deficits. This deficit spending and the Fed's unprecedented monetary stimulus have many investors worried about inflation or even hyperinflation.

I understand the concern. According to standard monetary economics, monetizing the debt and spending beyond your means is a recipe for inflation. We are, however, living in extraordinary times.

As quickly as the federal government is racking up new debts, the private sector—and particularly the financial sector—is actually paying back its debts faster. Consider **Figure 5.7**. Starting in the mid-1990s, the United States went on a debt binge. The financial sector was by far the biggest offender, followed by household mortgages. Of course, much of the financial sector debt is based on mortgages and derivatives of mortgages via the alphabet soup of mortgage-backed securities (MBS), collateralized mortgage obligations (CMO), and the now almost ridiculous sounding CMOs of CMOs, or CMO^2.

So, the financial sector bubble and the housing bubble were really one in the same. And with mortgage lending currently a fraction of what it used to be and the market for new mortgage derivative securities practically nonexistent, it should come as no surprise to see the total debt in these sectors falling. Banks and individual Americans alike are paying down existing debts and are not adding new ones.

Figure 5.8 has a way of putting the debt data in perspective. This chart shows the year-over-year change in debt by sector. As you can see, the deleveraging of the financial sector pretty well washes out the borrowing of the government.

Remember, in a credit-based economy, cash and debt are essentially the same thing. As the commercials remind us, "for the rest there is MasterCard." But a dollar used to pay down existing debts is a dollar that does not get spent in the economy. It is a destruction of purchasing power and an important reason why deflation, not inflation, will be with us for a long time to come. Quite simply, credit and therefore money is being destroyed faster than the government can create it.

If Japan's recent history is any guide—and you will soon see why it is—then the United States will likely run large budget deficits for years or even a decade or more, causing our national debt to expand to levels previously thought unimaginable. The only way I could see this not happening would be for another 1990s-caliber tax windfall or for massive government spending cuts, and I don't consider either realistic. The 1990's tax windfall was a result of the biggest economic boom this country had seen in a generation. And cutting government spending is politically hard. We all like the idea in principle, but when our favorite programs get targeted we tend to quickly change our minds. Despite this, I see overall levels of debt falling, continuing the trends of **Figures 5.7** and **5.8**.

As I noted earlier, in a credit-based economy, money and debt are essentially the same thing. Debts are being repaid, which is deflationary. But interestingly, the money supply is also shrinking, even as the monetary base remains outsized. Consider **Figure 5.9**, which tracks M3, the broadest measure of the money supply. M3 includes physical notes and coins, traveler's checks, checking accounts, savings accounts, certificates of deposits, and some forms of money market accounts.

So, even while the monetary base has more than doubled by the Federal Reserve since the onset of the crisis, the actual money in the real economy has shrunk.

You might be wondering how this is possible, and the answer is the fractional reserve banking system. For money to enter the financial system, it has to be loaned into existence. With credit standards higher these days, banks are less willing to lend, and consumers are less willing to borrow, particularly the aging Baby Boomers who have very little reason to borrow at this stage of their lives. As a result, the massive increase in the monetary base sits dormant in reserve in the banks' accounts at the Fed.

I've saved what is perhaps the most disturbing chart for last. Some readers might have heard the term "velocity of money" before, but most Americans have only a vague idea of what it means. It is a somewhat arcane term, but it is important in understanding what drives inflation and deflation. Money velocity is every bit as important as money supply in determining the price level.

In a nutshell, money velocity is exactly what it sounds like. It's the speed at which a dollar changes hands. Think of it this way. If Peter pays Paul a dollar for a snow cone and Paul in turn takes that same dollar and buys a Coke from Mary, there have been two dollars' worth of transactions. If instead Peter buys two snow cones from Paul for a combined two dollars and then Paul simply saves the money for a rainy day rather than buy a Coke from Mary, there has also been two dollars' worth of transactions. In the real economy, it does not matter if we spend multiple dollars or if we pass the same dollar around multiple times.

This is a concept that is a little hard to grasp at first, but perhaps it might be easier to tell it in a story:

It is a slow day in the small California town of Davis. The streets are deserted. Times are tough. Everybody is in debt and living on credit.

A tourist visiting the area drives through town, stops at the motel, and lays a $100 bill on the desk saying he wants to inspect the rooms upstairs to pick one for the night.

As soon as he walks upstairs, the motel owner grabs the bill and runs next door to pay his debt to the butcher.

The butcher takes the $100 and runs down the street to retire his debt to the pig farmer.

The pig farmer takes the $100 and heads off to pay his bill to his *supplier, the Co-op.*

The guy at the co-op takes the $100 and runs to pay his debt to a woman he owes money to that's staying at the hotel.

The woman rushes to the hotel and pays off her room bill with the hotel owner.

The hotel proprietor then places the $100 back on the counter so the traveler will not suspect anything.

At that moment the traveler comes down the stairs, states that the rooms are not satisfactory, picks up the $100 bill and leaves.

No one produced anything. No one earned anything. However, the whole town is now out of debt and now looks to the future with a lot more optimism.

And that, ladies and gentlemen, is how money velocity works. Money velocity is hard to accurately calculate and so often ends up being a "plug" number in economics equations.[2] Still, we can approximate it by dividing GDP by the monetary base (**Figure 5.10**).

In case anyone has lingering questions about why inflation has been muted for the past six years in spite of all the inflationary stimulus, Figure 5.10 should answer it. The pace of economic activity plummeted during the crisis and has yet to recover. The Fed made a lot of new money available, but no one seemed interested in spending it!

Without belaboring the point, in a following chapter I want to offer one final explanation for the rate of inflation or deflation: demographics. But first, I want to take a short trip across the Pacific—to Japan.

CHAPTER 6:

DEMOGRAPHICS AND PRICES

In Chapter 2, I discussed the basic mechanics of inflation and deflation with an emphasis on the recent financial crisis. In this chapter we will discuss various views of what drives changes in prices. Most views have at least some truth to them, but it is the demographic view that is the most compelling and relevant today. If inflation and deflation are common themes in this book, it is because I consider them to be extraordinarily important to us as investors.

The portfolio you should build for deflationary times is very different from one you should build for inflationary times, and making the wrong choice can cost you dearly, especially if you are on a fixed income. In deflationary times, assets that produce safe, predictable income are generally best. This would include bonds, preferred stock, annuities (fixed not variable) and even high-quality dividend-paying blue chip stocks. But in an inflationary environment, these kinds of assets get absolutely killed. If the cost of living rises due to inflation but your investment income does not, you get poorer every day. In an inflationary time, hard assets like gold, commodities, and real estate generally do best. But as you can imagine, during deflationary times when prices are falling, these kinds of assets are the last thing you want to own. Investors who loaded up on gold and silver during the inflationary 1970s saw much of their wealth evaporate during the 1980s when inflation fell.

With all of this in mind, let's jump into our discussion on the root causes of price changes.

There are two main schools of thought, Keynesian and Monetarist, pioneered by John Maynard Keynes and Milton Friedman, respectively. Other, less orthodox views have used demographics to explain inflation and deflation. Thus far, the best demographic arguments have been made by David Hackett Fischer and Gregory Clark for pre-industrial economies and by Harry S. Dent, Jr. for post-industrial, mass-affluent societies like ours today. Fed Chairman Ben Bernanke and Professor Jeremy Siegel—whom we mentioned in the last chapter—also offered some insights on the matter, and their views will be discussed. We'll examine each of these views in the pages that follow.

In Chapter 5, the charts I used to describe "good deflation," "bad deflation," and "demand-based inflation" were straight out of the Keynesian textbook. Demand-based inflation is called "demand-pull" inflation by Keynesians, but the gist is the same. When increases in aggregate demand (due to increased private and government spending) outstrip increases in aggregate supply, prices rise. It's exactly like an auction. Prices rise when there are more bidders for a given item. And, of course, the opposite is also true: Prices fall when there are fewer bidders.

The other form of inflation that Keynesians identify is "cost-push" inflation, also called "supply shock" inflation. For those who remember the gas shortages of the 1970s, that is what we are talking about here. Prices rise when there is a sudden disruption in supply that causes an unexpected shortage. This form of inflation tends to be the most destructive to the health of the economy, and thankfully it is relatively rare.

Either form of inflation can lead to what Keynes called the "price/wage spiral," in which workers get used to rising prices and thus demand higher wages. Of course, rising labor costs force companies to raise their prices further, creating a vicious cycle that can be difficult to break. This was the situation in the late 1970s. It took some of the most hawkish Fed action in history under Paul Volker and two deep recessions in the early 1980s to finally break it.

The other mainstream view of inflation and deflation is that of the Monetarist school, led by the late Milton Friedman. Friedman proposed that changes in the price level are almost purely effects of monetary policy by the Federal Reserve. One of Friedman's most quoted statements was: "*Inflation is always and everywhere a monetary phenomenon.*" In this line of thinking, if the Fed "prints" more money than is needed to make the economy function, the value of that money decreases and the price of everything rises. Hence, we have inflation. On the flip side, if the Fed fails to print enough money, we have a "shortage" of cash, and prices fall: deflation. This is loosely the view of Fed Chair Janet Yellen and her predecessors Ben Bernanke and Alan Greenspan, and there is definitely some truth to it. Central banks are certainly capable of creating artificial inflation or deflation. It wasn't that long ago that Brazil had an inflation rate of over 1,000% per year, and when referring to U.S. economic history both Friedman and Bernanke have mentioned that unnecessarily high interest rates by the Fed were a major contributing factor to the deflation of the Great Depression. Central banks can get monetary policy wrong in either direction, causing inflation or deflation as the case might be.

Friedman is correct to say that a central bank can affect the money supply. But his theory has one very large hole in it. A central bank cannot increase the velocity of money, or the frequency with which a dollar changes hands in the economy. As Keynes correctly pointed out, in the absence of underlying demand, stimulative monetary policy (a.k.a. printing more money) is akin to "pushing on a string." Simply having more money around does not guarantee that it will be spent.

Demographics: The Inflation of People

In his 1996 book *The Great Wave*, David Hackett Fischer describes the last 1,000 years of human history as a series of price revolutions caused by demographic shifts. The basic pattern goes something like this: Increases in productivity lead to social stability and higher real incomes, which encourages population growth. Population growth means more mouths to feed, which means the farming of marginal land to produce more food. Farming on lower-quality land reduces productivity, which leads to rising prices for food (inflation). Rising food prices leads to chaos and instability, which in turn leads to falling populations until a new equilibrium is found. And the cycle continues. A growing agrarian labor force leads to falling real wages, lower standards of living, unrest, substance abuse, illegitimate births, and a general breakdown of society. In this environment, medieval landlords were the only people to do well, as they benefited from rising rents on their land. This leads to greater social inequality, which usually results in political instability and a reduction in the birthrate. As population falls and marginal land is no longer used, productivity goes up, crop prices fall, real incomes go up, and returns on capital go down. This increases the wealth of the labor force but causes financial strain for landlords, resulting in greater equality between social classes.

So, in the pre-industrial world, life got much worse for the common man during inflationary times and actually quite a bit better during deflationary times. Meanwhile, the exact opposite was true for the landlords, or the rich. The propertied class did well during inflationary times and fell under severe financial distress during deflationary times. So, by this logic, we should welcome deflation, right? After all, if only a small minority of the ultra-affluent suffer, what's the big deal?

The problem with this argument is that today we all have a lot more in common with the medieval landlord than with the medieval peasant. In the modern, mass-affluent economy, virtually all of us have the trappings of the rich. We have mortgages to pay and assets to protect. We no longer live in the world of subsistence in which the affordability of food is the most pressing concern for most of humanity.

This brings us to the work of another economic historian, Gregory Clark, author of *A Farewell to Alms*. Clark explains at length the dynamics of the "Malthusian" economy, named after Thomas Malthus, the English demographer and thinker who predicted that mankind would face mass starvation by the middle of the 19th century. In the Malthusian world of scarcity, mankind survived at an equilibrium just slightly above the subsistence level. Any increase in productivity would result in higher incomes, which would result in higher birthrates. The increased number of people would push income back to the subsistence level. If, due to a famine, war, crop failure, etc., income fell below the subsistence level, people would have fewer children and would suffer higher mortality rates. The weakest among us would be the first to die until our populations thinned out enough to make subsistence living possible again. In this Darwinian world of "survival of the fittest," disease, pestilence, death and destruction were perversely the best friends of the healthy among us. If a bout of plague hit a given region and wiped out 30% of the population, all of the survivors saw their respective pieces of the income pie get 30% larger. Fewer mouths to feed meant more food for the rest of us!

Luckily, the Industrial Revolution pulled us out of this morbid cycle. For the first time in human history, ordinary people had the ability to generate real wealth and live in a society of abundance, not scarcity. In the industrial world, rising populations meant more production, better division of labor, more specialization, and higher standards of living. In the mass-affluent society that emerged, larger populations meant more consumers, more people to buy what you have to sell. The family, in the words of Brink Lindsey is his insightful book *The Age of Abundance*, became for the first time a unit of consumption rather than a unit of production.

Both Fischer and Clark take a view of inflation consistent with Keynes and the classical economists. Prices rise and fall as supply and demand shift. Like Keynes, these men focus mostly on the "demand side" of the equation, supply being limited to the arable land available to grow food. "Supply side" economics is meaningless in a pre-industrial agrarian world of low productivity growth. And Milton Friedman's contention that inflation is always a monetary phenomenon is simply not true. Yes, the governments of the pre-industrial era debased their currency by diluting the gold and silver content of their coins. This has been a recurring theme since the first kings issued the first coins. But this pre-industrial monetarism is clearly less significant than the demographic forces at work.

Inflation in the Era of Mass Affluence

Fischer and Clark's work is excellent at explaining why farm prices rose and fell centuries ago. But what about today, in the modern era?

In the early 1990s, Harry S. Dent, Jr. took the inflation/deflation demographic debate in an entirely new direction. Dent argued that in a developed, service-based economy such as the United States today, labor is by far the biggest and most significant "input" in the production process. In order for employees to be viable, they must produce more in output than they cost in wages. Unfortunately, new workers produce very little in their first few months or years, yet they still have to be paid. They also need a desk and a computer or machine tools and a hard hat, not to mention office or factory space and possibly even a company car or mobile phone. And I haven't even mentioned fringe benefits such as health insurance (which I cover in the next chapter) and continuing education classes that add to the cost of each employee.

This means that when a new employee is hired, the company's expenses instantly rise but with little or no change in production. When this happens on a large scale, we have inflation. And of course, inflation doesn't start at employment. Raising and educating young people requires a massive investment from both their parents and the government. Hence, young people are inflationary from birth (or even sooner, given the rising cost of pre-natal care) until they enter the workforce and start to produce more than they cost (typically two to three years after entry). We can even take this one step further: When a career woman becomes a mother and takes maternity leave, she is temporarily removed from her normal productive capacities at work. This means that the company continues to have expenses while getting no production. Not to mention the lost productivity of mothers and fathers alike from the sleepless nights of attending to a crying baby or a sick toddler. My son, Josh, may be years past that stage, but I remember those nights like they were yesterday. I could continue this train of thought almost indefinitely, but you get my point: Children are inflationary from birth until early career.

Of course, this is not a bad thing. Children are a necessary investment in the future. New workers eventually become highly productive, and their human capital becomes an asset to the company that hires them and to the country as a whole. Perhaps more importantly, fresh talent brings new ideas and innovations. Oftentimes, the full benefits of these innovations are not realized for decades. Consider personal computers. The key innovations in this product were made by Steve Jobs and Bill Gates by their respective companies in the early 1980s, but the resulting revolution in productivity did not happen until the mid-1990s. Companies and individuals invested millions (if not billions) of dollars before they began to truly realize a payoff.

In this context, inflation can be thought of as a means of financing new generations and the new technologies that they bring. Innovation and inflation go hand in hand.

Unfortunately for us, labor force growth actually goes negative in 2010 as Boomer retirements outnumber workforce entry by their children, the Echo Boomers. This implies that even in the absence of the debt deleveraging issues I described in Chapter 2, inflation would have ground to a halt. Naturally, this is not an exact measure. Baby Boomers could choose to work longer, which could postpone the workforce shrinkage. In the wake of the 2008 collapse, which wrecked the portfolios of many Boomers, this is exactly what we are seeing today. There could also be a shift in the percentage of women who choose to pursue gainful employment, which could shift the chart in either direction. Regardless, these changes would be marginal and the trend would remain the same. The main factor driving the deflationary forces in the years ahead is the retirement of the Boomers and a decrease in the workforce entry of their children. Fewer young professionals means less inflation.

But Isn't a Shrinking Workforce Inflationary?

The common view in academia is the demographic changes facing the country are inflationary. This view, explained most eloquently by Dr. Jeremy Siegel and former Federal Reserve Chairman Ben Bernanke, can be summarized like this:

As the Baby Boomers begin to retire, we will have comparatively fewer workers. This means that a smaller number of workers will have to work to support the consumption needs of the country. Fewer workers mean less production, or supply. If supply falls while demand remains the same, prices will have to rise as the marketplace reacts. Thus, we will have inflation. Furthermore, a shortage of labor could develop, which would force companies to raise wages in order to compete for workers, adding further inflationary pressure. The end result will be a form of 1970s-style stagflation, so the thinking goes.

While this view has its intuitive appeal, there are several flaws. I will debunk these flaws by using the example of a single extended family.

When a man and woman marry or begin to live together, they have certain economies of scale. Renting one apartment or making one mortgage payment is cheaper than two. Likewise, the couple shares one set of utility bills, furniture, linens, kitchen utensils and every other facet of modern life.

When the couple begins to have children, life gets a lot more expensive. Suddenly, that small apartment needs to be bigger, as does the car. In addition to their regular expenses, the new parents can also add Junior's baby food, clothes, medical bills, and day care to the list. Things only get worse as Junior ages. Soon, the parents find themselves paying for swimming lessons, band camp, and college prep classes.

At this stage in his life, Junior is an inflationary pressure on the household. He produces nothing of economic value, yet he consumes more and more, as all youngsters do—on Mom and Dad's tab. Luckily for Mom and Dad's finances, Junior eventually moves out and gets a job. About this time, however, Grandma retires and decides to move into Junior's old room at Mom and Dad's house.

In the Siegel/Bernanke model, Grandma is considered to be every bit as inflationary as Junior, which assumes that children and the retired are interchangeable parts. Both consume and neither produce. Therefore, both are inflationary, right?

Figure 7.1 Japan Nikkei Stock Index

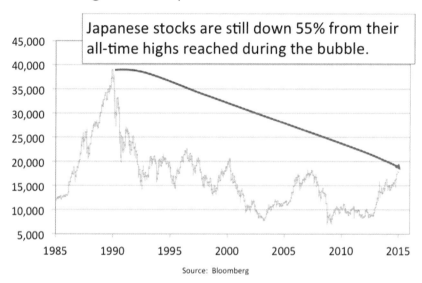

Source: Bloomberg

Figure 7.2 Japan Urban Land Index

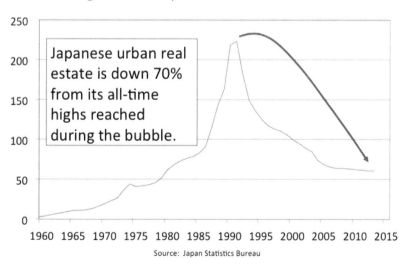

Source: Japan Statistics Bureau

Not so fast! Empirical evidence (and common sense) would tell us that a person's consumer spending is highly dependent on that person's age and stage of life, as I covered in Chapter 5. People today can be expected to spend more every year of their life until their late 40s or early 50s. With retirement in sight, people begin to consume less and save more. With the exception of health care, spending on virtually everything decreases in late career and retirement. Sure, Grandma has to eat, but she doesn't eat as much as a growing Junior, and Grandma isn't buying a new closet of clothes every six months, a basketball hoop, or the latest iPod. And she certainly isn't buying a new washer or dryer, a big-screen plasma TV, or driving 20,000 miles per year as a taxi service for a child. It is the purchase of these big-ticket durable goods that boosts aggregate demand, and consumers peak in their demand for these items much earlier than retirement. This is the fundamental flaw in the Siegel/Bernanke argument. An aging population full of retirees spends substantially less money (especially on the highly leveraged durable goods) and is deflationary, not inflationary.

Siegel and Bernanke's view is contrary to the logic of the economic historians mentioned above—Fischer, Clark and Dent—and to the recent real-life experience of Japan. All of the research described above makes a compelling point that falling (or aging) populations are deflationary. Yet the inflationary view persists and appears to be gaining acceptance. So there you have it. In this chapter, I brought out the academic "big guns" to drive home a couple very important points. First of all, inflation is not controlled by the Fed. The Fed is an important contributor, of course. But demographics are the real force to be reckoned with. And demographic trends support the view that deflation will be more of a threat than inflation. Any inflation in the years ahead should be mild.

There is one enormous exception to this, however. As I mentioned in the example of the extended family, we tend to spend a lot more money on health care as we age. So, even in a period of negligible overall consumer price inflation, demographic forces could cause significant inflation in certain subsectors of the economy, and perhaps none more than health care, so let's talk about it next.

Figure 7.3: Bank of Japan Discount Rate

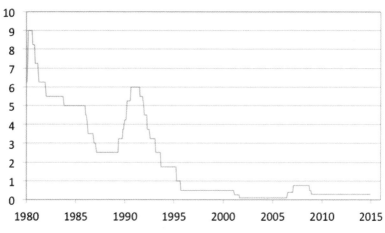

Source: Bank of Japan

Figure 7.4: Japan Monetary Base

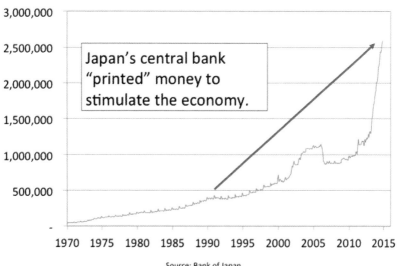

Japan's central bank "printed" money to stimulate the economy.

Source: Bank of Japan

Figure 7.5: Japan Money Supply % Change from Previous Year

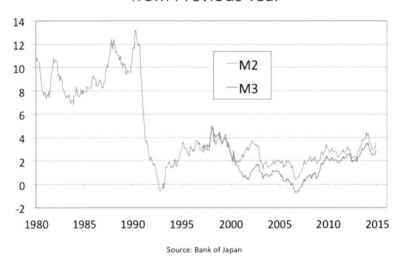

Source: Bank of Japan

Figure 7.6: Japan Government Debt as a % of GDP

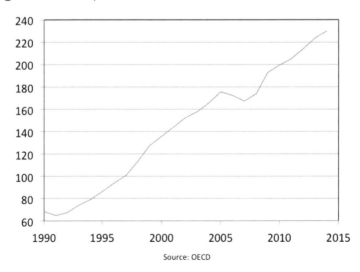

Source: OECD

Figure 7.7: Japan Inflation CPI Year-Over-Year % Change

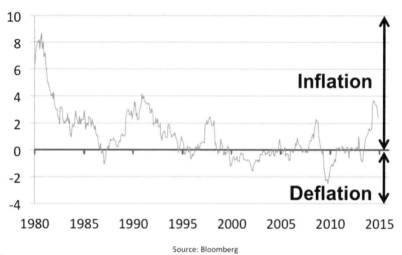

Source: Bloomberg

CHAPTER 7:

"I THINK I'M TURNING JAPANESE, I REALLY THINK SO"

The 1980 release of the Vapors song "Turning Japanese" had much more relevance than you might think. Believe it or not, Japan is the original poster child for a demographic cliff bringing down an economy. One line may sum it up best: Since 2011, there are more adult diapers being sold in Japan than baby diapers. With our 90 million Baby Boomers, it's easy to see how this scenario could be replayed here in the States. Let me explain…oh, by the way, sorry for getting that song stuck in your head.

Events never unfold in exactly the same manner twice. There are different people involved and different sets of circumstances. But, nevertheless, the stories tend to be remarkably similar. I bring this up because Japan went through a debt bubble and crisis two decades ago just like our own. It is scary how similar the two countries' situations are, and it certainly provides a sobering vision of our future.

Japan was the first modern "miracle" economy in the years following World War II. No country in history could match Japan's growth rates from the 1950s through the 1970s. In just two decades, Japan evolved from a largely agrarian country to an industrial powerhouse that rivaled the United States. By the 1980s, Americans suddenly found themselves struggling to compete with Japanese manufacturers of steel, automobiles and consumer electronics. The staid, conservative Swiss watch industry was decimated by upstarts like Japan's Seiko. East Asia appeared to be "re-colonized" by Japanese corporations. The world clamored to learn Japanese. All around the world, Japan, Inc. was on the offensive.

Think back to 1980s pop culture. Remember the sequel to Back

Figure 7.8: Japan Inflation Consumer Price Index

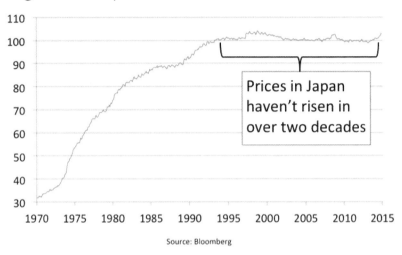

Prices in Japan haven't risen in over two decades

Source: Bloomberg

Figure 7.9: Japan Population Estimates

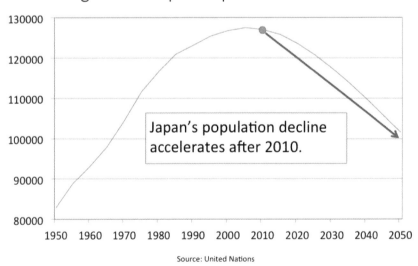

Japan's population decline accelerates after 2010.

Source: United Nations

to the Future in which Michael J. Fox gets to see a glimpse of his future? His boss was Japanese and was calling him on a video conference phone from Tokyo—reflecting the widespread belief at the time that we would all have Japanese bosses in just a few short years.

The Japanese stock market played its part in the affair (**Figure 7.1**). Share prices shot through the roof in the 1980s, and by the middle of the decade, they were in a speculative bubble. Between 1985 and 1990 the Nikkei tripled, hitting a high just shy of 40,000 in December of 1989.

Not to be outdone, the Japanese real estate bubble dwarfed that of the stock market (**Figure 7.2**). Home prices in Tokyo far outpaced incomes, making 100-year multigenerational mortgages a necessity. At its peak, Japanese property was worth four times that of the entire United States, and the area around the Imperial Palace alone was gauged to be more valuable than the state of California, Silicon Valley and all.

Those bubble days are long gone, and today we see a very different Japan. Japanese stocks and urban land are still down 55% and 70% respectively from their peak nearly two decades ago. And this is after the famed "Abenomics" policies of Japanese Prime Minister Shinzo Abe. Japan has spent the last 20 years in and out of recession, unable to gain any real momentum. So, what caused Japan to fall into this long, dark economic hibernation?

As you might guess, it was largely the falling desire of Japanese consumers. Low consumer demand due to the aging of the population meant low profits for Japanese companies, which in turn led to decreased hiring and even lower demand. A vicious cycle developed with no way out.

This phenomenon could have been easily predicted, however, if you simply knew where to look. Essentially, what the Japanese were going through was the natural demographic cycle of an aging country that spends less and saves more. The situation was exacerbated by an over-leveraged, over-indebted population.

Does this sound familiar? This scenario—lower demand, lower profits, lower production, lower demand—is clearly playing out the same way in the United States, beginning in the early 2000s, precipitating the last crash and lasting until about 2022.

But surely nothing like that could happen in the United States, many pundits insist. The Fed has effectively lowered the Federal Funds target rate to zero. The Bush and Obama administrations launched the biggest fiscal stimulus drive in history. Would this not save us from falling into a deflationary trap like Japan? Unfortunately, the historical precedent suggests it will not.

As the Japanese crisis wore on, the Bank of Japan cut interest rates from 6% to zero (**Figure 7.3**), essentially giving money away in the hopes that someone would spend it. In the standard monetarist formula, lowering interest rates spurs both consumption and investment. As the reward for saving money gets smaller, the incentive to spend it or invest it gets bigger. But a curious thing happened on the way to the fish market; interest rates dropped, but savings remained high. Consumer spending stayed flat and then fell. New investment in productive assets stalled; Japanese businesses already had more than enough capacity. In the 1930s, John Maynard Keynes likened this kind of situation to "pushing on a string." It could also be compared to herding cats. Injecting liquidity into the system and making money available to lend is useless if no one is interested in borrowing.

That did not stop Japan from trying, of course. The Bank of Japan aggressively monetized the county's debts, causing the monetary base to soar (**Figure 7.4**). As I suggested in the previous chapter, when the monetary base expands rapidly, the result is generally inflation or even hyperinflation. The German Weimar Republic of the 1920s comes to mind, which led to a little man with an odd little mustache who brought the entire world to the brink of ruin in World War II. But the Japanese economy resisted this convention. Even while the monetary base expanded, the growth rate of the money supply fell from over 12% to less than zero. "Plunged" (**Figure 7.5**) might be a better word. Sound familiar?

The Bank of Japan made credit available. But with the value of their loans having fallen significantly below the market price of the underlying collateral, Japanese banks were not interested in lending. They became "zombies," technically insolvent yet continuing to roll over existing loans, all the while absorbing loanable funds that might have been better put to use elsewhere.

Japan did not stop with central bank monetary policy, of course. The government launched countless expensive fiscal stimulus programs, most of which produced barely a ripple. Much like the Roosevelt administration during the Depression, the Japanese used massive government deficit spending to spur demand, but the Japanese did this on an even bigger scale. The once fiscally conservative Japanese government went on the largest public works spending spree in history, boosting its budget deficits and government debts to levels rarely seen in developed countries (**Figure 7.6**).

Today, Japan has 30 times the amount of land covered in concrete as the United States, adjusting for the size difference in the two countries, and over 2,800 river dams[3], but the Japanese version of the Tennessee Valley Authority could not possibly hope to spend enough money to compensate for a lack of private consumer spending.

Take another look at **Figure 7.6**. Japan's government debt is now 230% of the country's annual GDP. This is unprecedented for an industrialized country, and it will be a major impediment for a very long time.

I'll return to this theme in a later chapter, offering insight from Harvard professor Kenneth Rogoff and University of Maryland professor Carmen Reinhart. But for now, let us continue our discussion of inflation.

One might think that Japan's government spending binge would have stimulated demand and ignited the desired inflation. Nothing could be further from the truth.

For any readers who continue to believe that the U.S. government's actions will lead to inflation (and are busily selling stocks to buy gold), take a long look at **Figures 7.7** and **7.8**. The Japanese government wanted inflation, and couldn't make it happen. As you can see in **Figure 7.7**, Japan started to have severe disinflation in late 1990, which fell into full-blown deflation by 1995. Japan has struggled to rise out of deflation ever since.

Figure 7.8 is an index of Japan's price level. Prices in Japan haven't risen in 18 years. The last time Japan had sustained inflation, Bill Clinton was still the governor of Arkansas!

Of course, the United States is not Japan. This is a different country in a different decade with a host of unique issues. But returning to the Mark Twain quote, history does rhyme. If I have inundated you with charts in the last two chapters, it is to drive home this important point. Our situation today is similar to that of Japan two decades ago, but not the same.

In both countries there was a debt-fueled bubble in property that was followed by a colossal bust and a prolonged period of economic stagnation. I believe that the situation here is grave, but I want to stress that I do not believe that it is quite as bad as Japan. Even more importantly, I want to make it clear that there are ways to make money in this market that do not involve a great degree of risk. The 1930s was arguably the worst decade for stocks this country has ever seen, yet during that period the most millionaires in American history were created. And there were stretches of multiple years in the 1930s when the stock market actually did quite well.

18 years from now, I do not expect us to still be suffering from deflation. We will have our problems, of course. The funding issues of Social Security and Medicare and the ballooning federal debt are not going away any time soon. But Japan has issues that we simply do not have. Japan's population is aging rapidly and is actually shrinking as deaths exceed births (**Figure 7.9**). Imagine the difficulty

of running a retail-oriented business in Japan or even a restaurant. Every year, the base of potential customers gets smaller, and those that are left are older and less likely to buy anything. This is a slow-motion train wreck happening before our very eyes.

Japan will almost certainly collapse in one way or another. The government has run debts that it can never hope to repay, and the citizenry is slowly dying of old age. Currently their debt is in excess of 230% of GDP. This has forced S&P to cut Japan's credit rating to AA-, four marks below the best AAA rating. The only way out of the pending debt crisis is to devalue the debt through inflation. The problem with this is that inflation hurts the elderly far worse than anyone else due to their reliance on savings and pension payments, and Japan has the highest percentage of elderly citizens of any country in the world—elderly people who vote and who would, no doubt, punish any politician who wrecked their retirement dreams. As I have made painstakingly clear, Japan has also attempted to generate inflation for 20 years now and has failed.

I do understand that there are many who believe that the United States is also heading for hyperinflation. However, Japan is almost 20 years into its crisis, and as much as it is trying to create inflation, it hasn't happened yet. It is entirely possible that the United States will succumb to an inflationary spiral at some point. But if Japan is our guide, it will not happen any time soon.

"This time is different," is a common reply I hear when I use historical examples. But is it really?

The next chapter is dedicated to debunking a certain kind of denial I call the "this time is different" syndrome. If you are making the correct comparisons, events today are not at all different from those in the past.

The good news is that by virtue of being here today, we humans have proven that we persevere. Crises are not fun, but we do survive them and life goes on. The bad news is that history suggests we have a rough road in front of us.

What About Abenomics?

I have to give credit to Japanese Prime Minister, Shinzo Abe. In another life, he might have gone down in history as Japan's Ronald Reagan or Margaret Thatcher. But try as he might, it's not going to happen.

There were three "arrows" in Abe's plans to revitalize Japan: aggressive fiscal stimulus from government spending, aggressive monetary stimulus via new and exciting forms of quantitative easing from the Bank of Japan, and reform of Japan's tax code and regulatory red tape to make investing in Japan easier and more profitable.

The first two arrows—and particularly the quantitative easing program—were wildly successful in pushing down the value of the yen and in reviving the animal spirits in the Japanese stock market. But their effects on the real economy were mixed at best, and I would argue that over the long term they will make not one iota of difference. Japan will never get its economic mojo back. Its aging and shrinking demographics all but guarantee that Japan will eventually slide into oblivion.

And as for the third arrow, I expect its effects even in the short term to be virtually nil.

Let's take a look. At 35.6%, Japan has the second-highest corporate tax rate in the world after the United States, which tops out at about 40% after allowing for state and local levies. Yes, not even the notoriously high-taxing French extort as much money from their companies; France tops out at about 33%.

Details have not been released, but early estimates suggest that Japan's corporate tax rate could fall to as low as 20%.

So, given the high current tax burden faced by Japanese companies, a reduction in the tax rate should mean an investment boom in Japan, right?

All else equal, yes. But alas, all else is not equal. Return on investment in Japan is low by global standards due to existing overcapacity and, in any event, Japan already has some of the highest levels of capital spending in the G7. Japanese companies already invest too much in capital spending, and a lot of it is uneconomic and wasteful. And while a lower tax bill might boost corporate profits and give Japanese equities a jolt, it's hard to see this unleashing a Reagan or Thatcher-style economic transformation given the rest of Japan's baggage.

Remember, Japan is the oldest country in the world with a quarter of its population already over the age of 65. Japan's population peaked seven years ago at 128 million and hasn't stopped shrinking since– Japan has about a million fewer citizens every year. By 2060, the Japanese government estimates that Japan's population will have shrunk to 87 million people, and 40% will be over 65.

In a modern consumer economy, an aging and shrinking population is devastating to growth. Fewer people mean fewer consumers—and less spending, unless you believe that a smaller consumer base will somehow buy more goods and services per capita. That could only happen if real income per capita outpaced population decline, which is a scenario that is hard to envision. Rising income would only come with rising production per capita, which, again, only makes sense in a stable or growing population.

Likewise, older consumers buy much less than those in middle age (certain items like healthcare notwithstanding). So again, an aging and shrinking population means less spending and slower economic growth.

This is why Japan's recessionary conditions are not cyclical but structural. Think about it: Why would builders build new homes if there are fewer people to live in them? Why would companies invest in new capacity if there are fewer consumers to sell to?

Hey, I'm a believer in small government, and I'm generally very favorable towards tax cuts. I see nothing wrong with Abe's decision to lower taxes in a bid to make Japan more competitive. But let's get realistic. It's not going to be a game changer.

The third arrow will also have policies aimed at getting Japan's women back to work. Japan currently has one of the lowest female labor force participation rates in the developed world. Details are yet to be released, but again, it's hard to see this having a big impact. And it's not clear that it would fix Japan's biggest problem of all: Its lack of children! Unless Japan can somehow convince its women to have large, four to five children families and institute economic policies that would somehow make that affordable in modern Japan (never mind changing social attitudes keeping women at home that have endured for centuries) and somehow enable them to do all of that while also pursuing a fulfilling career, it's hard to see any of this mattering much.

After an initial spurt of growth, Japan is sputtering again. Japanese GDP shrank by 1.6% in the third quarter of 2014 after shrinking by 7.3% in the second quarter. The culprit? Japanese consumer spending, which was much weaker than expected. Consumer spending makes up about 60% of Japanese gross domestic product, and Japanese consumers have snapped their wallets shut following a sales tax hike earlier this year.

The only surprise here should be that economists didn't see this coming. Japan has seen GDP fall in three of the past four quarters. The only quarter that saw growth—the first quarter of 2014—was an outlier skewed by the pending sales tax hike. Japanese shoppers went on a spending spree in
the first quarter in order to avoid the new sales tax.

The media is calling this a failure of Abenomics, and it is—sort of. But I would argue it goes much deeper than that. The bigger failure is that economists thought Abenomics ever had any chance of success. Of the 59 quarters that have passed since 2000, the Japanese economy spent 21 of them shrinking.

And in many of the quarters that had GDP growth, the "growth" is mostly a result of poor comps from the previous year. It's not hard to show "growth" when your previous year's results were awful.

A little quantitative easing (OK, a lot of quantitative easing in the case of Abenomics) is not going fix an economy this broken. Hey, I'll give credit to Prime Minister Shinzo Abe and to Bank of Japan Governor Haruhiko Kuroda for making the effort; at current exchange rates, Japan's quantitative easing program is about three times bigger than Ben Bernanke and Janet Yellen's "QE infinity" adjusted for the size of Japan's economy. Kuroda is buying bonds at a rate equal to 16% of Japan's entire economy, every year, until further notice. That's a big deal. Unfortunately, it wasn't big enough to kick start Japan's economy.

I've droned on about Japan long enough. The good news is that I don't see our demographic challenges being anything close to Japan's. But I tell the Japan story to drive an important point home. If you want to know what to expect from an economy, look to demographics. Good, bad or ugly, they will tell you what to expect. And in the U.S., demographics point to a very bright future once we get into the 2020s. But between now and then, be careful. We'll probably have another recession or two, and it makes sense to stay nimble.

CHAPTER 8:

THE SCARIEST FOUR WORDS IN FINANCE – THIS TIME IS DIFFERENT

King Solomon had it all figured out when, more than 3,000 years ago, he wrote, "There is nothing new under the sun." [4] He was a tired old man who had seen it all and had the good sense and humility to realize that his circumstance wasn't all that unique. You can imagine him staring out of his palace and asking himself, "Is there anything of which one can say, 'Look! This is something new? It was here already, long ago; it was here before our time.'"

It's a shame so few have heeded his observation; otherwise we might have avoided the housing bubble and meltdown of the 2000s—and every other financial crisis in human history.

In their recent book, *This Time Is Different*[5], Carmen Reinhart and Kenneth Rogoff draw the same conclusion as old Solomon. This time it's not different. It never is, and it probably never will be. As they state in the introduction, "Our basic message is simple: We have been here before. No matter how different the latest financial frenzy or crisis always appears, there are usually remarkable similarities with past experience from other countries and from history." The names, faces and financial instruments might change, but the plot does not. And neither does the ending.

I am a big believer in the repetitiveness of history. There are generational cycles, as Strauss and Howe have outlined in their work.[6] There is the boom and bust cycle of the economy, as explained by various economists, including John Maynard Keynes (who coined the phrase "animal spirits"), Friedrich von Hayek, and Joseph Schumpeter. There are cycles in stock and commodities markets as well.

The persistent occurrence of boom and bust cycles has been noted in Charles Kindleberger's book *Manias, Panics, and Crashes: A History of Financial Crises,* and in Charles Mackay's classic *Extraordinary Popular Delusions and the Madness of Crowds*, among others. What separates Reinhart and Rogoff's efforts from those of their predecessors is the sophistication of the delivery. Kindleberger and Mackay take a narrative approach, telling the story of each financial mania like a play-by-play announcer and noting similarities among them. Reinhart and Rogoff instead take a quantitative approach, building their analysis from a massive database that "encompasses the entire world and goes back as far as 12 century China."

From this database they can tell that that, on average, **government debt rises by 86% during the three years following a banking crisis**. So, while the Obama administration's record deficits may be unsettling, they are certainly nothing new in history. Reinhart and Rogoff point out that the increase in government debt is a much better gauge of the severity of a crisis than the explicit cost of bailouts alone. The increase in government debt reflects both explicit costs and the damage done to the real economy, seen in lower tax receipts. We are seeing this today at all levels of government—from Washington, DC, to local neighborhood homeowners' associations.

In this chapter, we're going to take a look at some of Reinhart and Rogoff's findings in an attempt to keep the current crisis in perspective. Their book has *far* too much information for us to cover in one short chapter, but I'll attempt to glean the most important parts for our purposes.

It Starts With Debt

In previous chapters I have focused heavily on the role of debt in the recent crisis and on the ongoing, multi-decade crisis in Japan. Reinhart and Rogoff would appear to agree:

> *If there is one common theme to the vast range of crises we consider in this book, it is that excessive debt accumulation,*

whether it be by the government, banks, corporations, or consumers, often poses greater systemic risks than it seems during a boom….

Such large-scale debt buildups pose risks because they make an economy vulnerable to crises of confidence, particularly when debt is short term and needs to be constantly refinanced. Debt-fueled booms all too often provide false affirmation of a government's policies, a financial institution's ability to make outsized profits, or a country's standard of living. Most of these booms end badly. Of course, debt instruments are crucial to all economies, ancient and modern, but balancing the risk and opportunities of debt is always a challenge, a challenge policy makers, investors, and ordinary citizens must never forget.

To illustrate how debt makes crises significantly more serious, the authors consider the case of the tech bubble and bust in 2001. While the amount of wealth destruction in the market crash was enormous and had a real effect on the retirement plans of millions of Americans, the overall damage to the economy was minor. We had a run-of-the-mill recession in 2001, which was worsened by the September 11 terror attacks. But not even the destruction of the Twin Towers, in the heart of America's financial center, could rival the damage done to the economy by the mortgage debt crisis that hit just six years later.

As Reinhart and Rogoff write, "What is certainly clear is that again and again, countries, banks, individuals and firms take on excessive debt in good times without enough awareness of the risks that will follow when the inevitable recession hits."

Here, the authors echo Hyman Minsky, whose work has enjoyed a comeback in recent years. Minsky's pet theory was the *Financial Instability Hypothesis*.[7] Minsky believed that financial stability led to its own demise. During healthy economic times, borrowers and lenders alike let their guard down, lured by rising asset prices and a lack of volatility. As banks lend more and more to eager borrowers, asset prices rise, often to inflated bubble levels. Eventually, the debt-fueled bubble becomes unsustainable, and the whole thing collapses like a house of cards. Only afterward do lenders and borrowers regain the conservatism that originally allowed for stability—and the cycle continues.

Sound familiar? Lending standards for a new mortgage are stiff today, after the crisis. It's like a never-ending cycle of closing the barn door after the horse has already bolted.

On Black Swans

Nassim Nicholas Taleb's pet phrase, "black swan," is well known in financial circles, although most people have only a murky idea as to what it means. A black swan is a high-impact, low probability event. It's something that you would never expect to happen, so when it does happen, it's a big deal.

However, as Taleb points out repeatedly in his work, black swans are not all that uncommon. In fact, they are an all too common occurrence in financial markets.

Reinhart and Rogoff, although they never use the phrase "black swan," arrive at the same end. They conclude that "rare" events are often not all that rare when viewed in a longer historical context.

Reinhart and Rogoff write,

> *Above all, our emphasis is on looking at long spans of history to catch sight of "rare" events that are all too often forgotten, although they turn out to be far more common and similar than people seem to think….*
>
> *An event that was rare in that twenty-five-year span may not be all that rare when placed in a longer historical context. After all, a researcher stands only a one-in-four chance of observing a "hundred-year flood" in twenty-five years' worth of data.*

Ironically, the historical crisis that most resembles our current one is the 1907 panic—which hit pretty close to exactly one hundred years before the 2008 meltdown.

Financial Crises By the Numbers

In their cross-sectional study, Reinhart and Rogoff dissect the anatomy of a financial crisis and find three common characteristics:

Asset market collapses are deep and prolonged. Declines in real housing prices average 35% stretched out over six years, whereas stock bear market declines average 56% over three and a half years.Interestingly, the current crisis is atypical in that the housing and stock market declines came much faster and harder than the average. Of course, the bubble in housing prices preceding the crisis was more than three times larger than average, implying that this one is likely to have further to go. As Reinhart and Rogoff point out, Japan is also a notable exception to the averages. Japan's housing and stock market declines have been virtually uninterrupted for two decades.

the aftermath of a banking crisis generally will include large declines in output and employment. The unemployment rate rises

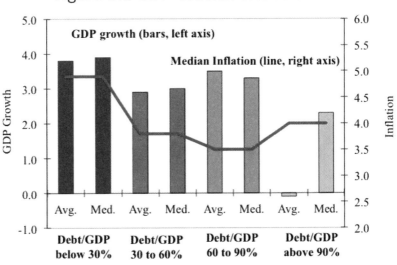

Figure 8.1 GDP Growth With Debt

Source: Reinhart and Rogoff 2010

an average of seven percentage points during the downward phase of the cycle, which lasts on average more than four years. Output (GDP) falls more than nine% on average over roughly two years. This shows that, in general, employment is a lagging indicator.

The U.S. is pretty close to the mark in unemployment, up roughly 6% to just shy of 10%. GDP decline has been nowhere near the 9% average, at least not yet. Let us hope it doesn't get there.

Finally, as mentioned earlier, government debts explode during a financial crisis, rising an average of 86% in real terms in the major post–World War II episodes. Currently, gross U.S. federal debt is up roughly 40%. This number implies that the U.S. government still has quite a bit of deficit spending to do.

Remember, these numbers are averages, which implies that roughly half of the crises in recorded history were more severe than these numbers would suggest. The sheer size of the American housing boom indicates that the bust we are now in could have some staying power.

But isn't the economy recovering? Of course it is. However, it's recovering from very low levels, and demand remains far below the pre-crisis highs. Demographic trends also suggest a rocky road ahead.

Hey, I'm not a doom and gloomer. And I'm the first one to point out that the economy has enjoyed a nice spurt of growth over the past six years. But I think we'd all agree that the growth has been fragile and uneven… and it always felt like it could slip away in a heartbeat. And this is what I expect to see going forward. Growth that is real but fragile and prone to periodic stalling.

Growth in a Time of Debt

After the publication of Reinhart and Rogoff's This Time Is Different, the authors did a 2010 follow-up white paper titled "Growth in a Time of Debt."[8]

With all of the talk of "double dip" recession in the news, Reinhart and Rogoff's paper is a timely analysis. We will find out soon enough whether the United States has technically entered recession again or if we narrowly avoid it with a period of very slow growth. It's my view that the entire discussion is an exercise in futility, comparable to the debate among medieval Catholic theologians who argued passionately about how many angels could balance on the head of a pin.

Whether reported GDP contracts or expands modestly, the basic fundamentals have not changed. We still have a financial system dominated by large banks with impaired balance sheets that are unable or unwilling to lend. We still have a housing sector that would appear highly susceptible to further declines if mortgage rates were to rise even slightly. And we still have the largest generation in history—the Baby Boomers—who need desperately to downsize their lives and save for retirement.

When GDP numbers are released, they tell us what happened last quarter. How, exactly, is this useful information?

Of particular concern these days is the rate of growth in the national debt. As a result of the bailouts and the collapse in tax receipts, the Federal debt had ballooned to $17.8 trillion by 2014, $12.8 trillion of which is held by the public. There is genuine worry that this expansion of debt will lead to financial instability and will have long-term effects on economic growth. As I mentioned earlier, in This Time is Different, Reinhart and Rogoff found that central government debt rises on average by about 86% after the crisis. Well, we actually exceeded that figure. Government debt is p by about 98% since the end of 2007.

Unlike most economic historians, who take a narrative approach to compare past crises to the present, Reinhart and Rogoff use a quantitative approach. There is no "fluff" in their analysis; it is based on cold, hard statistics.

The two academics compiled a new database covering 44 countries and spanning about hundred years. The dataset incorporates over 3,700 annual observations and, per Reinhart and Rogoff, "covers a wide range of political systems, institutions, exchange rate arrangements, and historic circumstances."

In exploring the relationship between government debt and economic growth the authors made some interesting observations.

> *The relationship between government debt and real GDP growth is weak for debt/GDP ratios below a threshold of 90% of GDP. Above 90 percent, median growth rates fall by one percent, and average growth falls considerably more. We find that the threshold for public debt is similar in advanced and emerging economies.*

> *Emerging markets face lower thresholds for external debt (public and private)—which is usually denominated in a foreign currency. When external debt reaches 60% of GDP, annual growth declines by about two percent; for higher levels, growth rates are roughly cut in half.*

> *There is no apparent link between inflation and public debt levels for the advanced countries as a group. The story is entirely different for emerging markets, where inflation rises sharply as debt increases.*

It is easy enough to understand why debt starts to crimp growth once it gets sufficiently high. Eventually, in order to appease lenders, taxes have to rise or spending has to slow. Both are contractionary to the economy.

The other solution is that governments will intentionally ignite inflation as a way to make existing debts shrink in real terms. This makes intuitive sense, and indeed it would appear that Ben Bernanke was attempting to do exactly that when he doubled the monetary base in 2008 and early 2009. But as I explained at length in prior chapters, deflation, not inflation, is a more likely scenario. The continued deleveraging of the private sector, prolonged by the Baby Boomers passing their peak spending years, will negate the inflationary policies of the Fed.

Reinhart and Rogoff's data would appear to support my view. Figure 8.1, which is somewhat hard to interpret at first glance, compares GDP growth (bars) and inflation (line) by various debt "buckets." The median inflation rate, at 4%, is considerably lower for high-debt countries (those with debt/GDP of over 90%) vs. low-debt countries (those with debt/GDP of less than 30%). Using the average instead of the median, we actually have mild deflation for a high-debt country. This is certainly the case in Japan today.

One question begs to be asked: Why is 90% the threshold?

Why does growth stall at 90% and not, say, 50% or 180%? Rogoff and Reinhart have no definitive answers to this question. Their data tells them what is; it does not tell them why.

We can, however, draw one, big meaningful conclusion from all of this. A rigorous empirical analysis of past financial crises would support my view that the coming years will be marked by slow economic growth and the persistent threat of deflation. That is, unless "this time is different."

Complexity and Collapse

On a related note, I want to mention an interesting article published by Niall Ferguson, the author of The Ascent of Money. Ferguson published an article in Foreign Affairs titled "Complexity and Collapse"[9] that ties in nicely with Reinhart and Rogoff's work. Ferguson's focus is on "imperial overstretch," and that is a topic outside of the scope of this book, but the article's insights on debt are instructive. Ferguson writes,

> There is no better illustration of the life cycle of a great power than The Course of Empire, a series of five paintings by Thomas Cole that hang in the New York Historical Society… In The Course of Empire, he beautifully captured a theory of imperial rise and fall to which most people remain in thrall to this day.
>
> Each of the five imagined scenes depicts the mouth of a great

river beneath a rocky outcrop. In the first, The Savage State, a lush wilderness is populated by a handful of hunter-gatherers eking out a primitive existence at the break of a stormy dawn. The second picture, The Arcadian or Pastoral State, is of an agrarian idyll: the inhabitants have cleared the trees, planted fields, and built an elegant Greek temple. The third and largest of the paintings is The Consummation of Empire. Now, the landscape is covered by a magnificent marble entrepôt, and the contented farmer-philosophers of the previous tableau have been replaced by a throng of opulently clad merchants, proconsuls, and citizen-consumers. It is midday in the life cycle. Then comes Destruction. The city is ablaze, its citizens fleeing an invading horde that rapes and pillages beneath a brooding evening sky. Finally, the moon rises over the fifth painting, Desolation. There is not a living soul to be seen, only a few decaying columns and colonnades overgrown by briars and ivy.

Popular sentiment would suggest we are somewhere in the late stages of "Consummation of Empire" or early stages of "Destruction." In any event, the view is that we are in for a long, protracted downfall as debt and bad demographics create roadblocks to a sustainable recovery.

Ferguson would argue that this is a fundamentally flawed way to look at history. History does not follow long cycles of rise and fall. Instead it is "arrhythmic—at times almost stationary, but also capable of accelerating suddenly, like a sports car." Collapse does not happen over time but comes suddenly, "like a thief in the night."

Ferguson suggests that great powers and empires (and I would suggest modern industrial economies) are complex systems that operate somewhere between order and disorder, "on the edge of chaos." Such systems—like Japan's economy, for example—can appear to be stable even while they are quietly and constantly deteriorating behind the scenes.

At some point, however, complex systems reach a *"tipping point,"* to use a term coined by Malcolm Gladwell. A very small trigger—the proverbial straw that breaks the camel's back—can set off a "phase transition from a benign equilibrium to a crisis."

Ferguson uses several examples from history to show that societies do not typically follow a slow decline. The destruction of Rome, an empire that lasted for centuries, happened in just a few short decades. The Ottoman and Hapsburg Empires too collapsed almost overnight. As more recent examples, Ferguson uses the British Empire and the Soviet Union. In retrospect, it seems obvious that Britain's global empire was unsustainable. After all, one of the rallying cries of the American Revolution was that an island had no authority to rule a continent. Yet was the impending collapse of the British Empire obvious to anyone in the decades before it happened? Britain was on the winning side of both world wars, but less than a decade after the end of World War II, she had lost substantially her entire empire. Similarly, it is easy for us today to argue that communism was doomed to fail in the Soviet Union. But ask the Baby Boomers if it was obvious to them when, as children, many of them practiced hiding under their desks in the event of a Soviet bombing of America.

I had the good fortune to visit the Soviet Union in 1984 when I was attending University of London. It wasn't easy for an American to travel there then, but I joined up with a group of British students. It was clear that their market was absolutely primitive in comparison to ours. There were barely any cars on the road, with most belonging to party officials. The technology was archaic, and a copy of Playboy magazine or just a few western cigarettes were valuable currency. Regardless, there were still no signs of obvious fracture. It wasn't pretty, but it appeared solid and stable. Nobody could have guessed that within just a few short years, the "Evil Empire" would collapse with breathtaking speed.

As Ferguson points out, historians love to tell history as narrative story, but in doing so they minimize the complexity of the real world. They make outcomes appear obvious in retrospect when at the time they were not obvious at all. This is what Nassim Taleb called *"the narrative fallacy"* in The Black Swan. Post hoc, ergo propter

SURFING THE RETIREMENT TSUNAMI

hoc. "After this, therefore because of this," or in other words, "if it happened this way, it had to happen this way."

I want to repeat something for emphasis: I am not a "doom and gloomer" who forecasts the fall of America. Not at all. I believe that we have difficult years ahead of us, but collapse—if it happens—is not something that I foresee happening in this lifetime. We might scale back our foreign policy ambitions—or we might not. But economic collapse strikes me as unlikely.

I'm not so sure about Japan, however. Using Ferguson's terms, Japan is in a state of stable equilibrium. The country's demographics are crumbling and government debt continues to expand at an alarming rate. But life is going on as usual for most Japanese. The financial system is still functioning. In fact, Japanese bond yields are still near record lows, and the yen remains a relatively strong currency.

But how long can this continue? According to Reinhart and Rogoff, debt begins to significantly crimp economic growth once it hits 90% of GDP. Japan is currently at 200%, and growth has certainly stalled.

It remains to be seen what the endgame for Japan will be. But if Ferguson's analysis holds, Japan's collapse, if or when it happens, will be much quicker and more abrupt that anyone expects. Holders of Japanese yen should keep that in mind.

Arenal Volcano. The view to my left as my world was blowing up on my laptop to the right.

Repelling down the Fortuna Waterfall.

Don Benigno himself at his cigar factory, showing off that his cigars could stand on its ash.

111

Diving the deep blue waters of Cocos Island, Costa Rica.

Hammerhead Shark tossed into a frenzy from the plastic water bottle trick. This picture made me realize the market was as dangerous as this shark and gave me the idea for the title and cover of this book.

113

With my mother and Josh watching the Blue Angels in San Francisco Bay. She always shares her words of wisdom when I need it most.

About to hit the depths for a wreck dive with dad and little Josh. Dad has great business savvy and always has good advice for me in tough situations.

CHAPTER 9:

I WILL GLADLY PAY YOU TUESDAY FOR A TRILLION DOLLARS TODAY

Debt is as old as human interaction, and has probably been used since the very beginning of the world's oldest profession.

What do you do when you're in debt and can't pay your bills? That's easy. You take out more debt until the bank shuts you off and you are forced to move to a van down by the river. However if you're a nation, then a whole lot more options are available to you, so you keep on going until you have the granddaddy of all debt bubbles.

The Popeye cartoons may have been comic relief during the depression when the ever hungry Wimpy would regularly utter his famous phrase "I will gladly pay you Tuesday for a hamburger today", but he also signified the common use of borrowing in American life. In fact, borrowing has been an American institution since the birth of America.

During the American Revolution, the Continental Congress solicited accepted loans from France. However, paying off these debts incurred proved to be one of the major challenges of the new nation state. Although the new U.S. Government tried to pay off these debts in a timely manner, doing so proved difficult and was often a source of great diplomatic tension.

The newly formed congress had two options: print more money or borrow more money to meet the budget deficit. Although it did both, it primarily relied on printing more money, which led to hyperinflation. The U.S. Congress didn't have any authority to levy taxes on its citizens. Not to mention that it would have been wildly unpopular to do so having just gone to war with Britain over the issue of unjust taxation.

Debt is by no means an American conundrum. If you think that Fed Chair Janet Yellen is unpopular, consider the tragic case of Takahashi Korekiyo, who served as Bank of Japan governor from 1911-1913 and as finance minister and prime minister in the 1920s and 1930s.

Mr. Takahashi helped to pull Japan out of the Great Depression with aggressive monetary stimulus (or "quantitative easing," in the popular jargon of today) and deficit spending. Unfortunately, like a man who joins the mafia, he found that he couldn't get out. The Japanese economy had become dependent on stimulus, and when Mr. Takahashi finally decided to risk it by tightening monetary policy and cutting government spending, he was assassinated by a group of rogue army officers.

Janet Yellen is at little risk of meeting such a fate, though there are

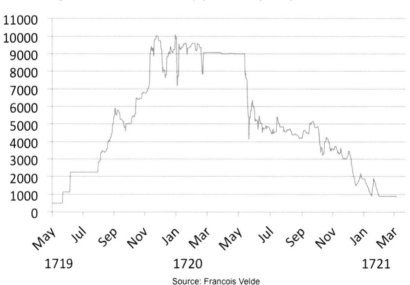

Figure 9.1: Mississippi Company Share Price

Source: Francois Velde

certainly plenty in Congress who would love to see her kicked out of the job. If certain members of the Tea Party had their way, the Chairman might meet the fate of John Law, the Scottish adventurer who, as France's first central banker, became the most powerful man in international finance—and the wealthiest man in the world—before having to flee penniless into exile and obscurity.

In the last chapter, we took a look at historical financial crises and made general comments about what happens during the bubble and the bust that follows. In this chapter, I want to recount the unfortunate story of the first major debt-fueled bubble and bust in Western history—the **Mississippi Land Scheme**.

John Law presided over the Mississippi Land Scheme, which was abetted by the creation of the first modern central bank in Europe, the French Banque Generale (later re-christened the Banque Royale). Law was an interesting character—a gentleman gambler with a taste for wealth, wine, women and power. His financial career began in the gaming halls of Europe after escaping a death sentence in England for killing a man in 1694, allegedly over the affections of a woman.

One might ask, how did this murdering degenerate come to control the financial destiny of France, then the most powerful nation in Europe? It was a long, circuitous path.

John Law was born in 1671 to an Edinburgh goldsmith. Goldsmiths were the foundation of the early European banking system, performing basic deposit and lending functions; they would take deposits of gold coin and issue paper certificates, which could be redeemed at any time for the gold they represented.

Learning the basic tricks of the trade from his father—and having a gift for calculating odds that made him dangerous in Europe's casinos—Law was exceptionally well positioned for a career in finance.

Law spent nine years on the run in Continental Europe after escaping

England and amassed a small fortune before returning to Scotland. (English warrants were not honored in Scotland at the time.) The Scotland that Law returned to was in the midst of a crisis after a disastrous colonial venture in Panama that wiped out the savings of much of the country's citizenry. Law's proposal to get the Scottish economy moving again—which was defeated by the Scottish parliament—was the issuance of paper money backed by the land owned by the government.

You see, monetary conditions in the wake of the crisis were extraordinarily tight. Given that there was a shortage of physical gold (as most of it was lost in the Panama debacle), banks and private citizens alike were hoarding what little cash they did have. The money supply was diminished and the velocity of money was in free fall. (Sound familiar? A collapse in the velocity of money is a common occurrence in nearly all post-bubble crises, and the American housing and debt crisis of 2008 was no exception.)

Law believed that paper money was preferable to gold or silver coinage for several reasons. Paper money is highly portable and

Figure 9.2: Long-Term Stock Prices

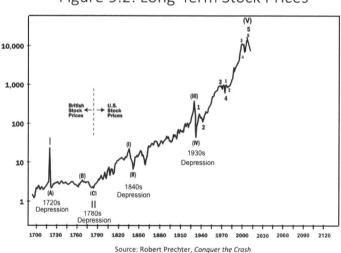

Source: Robert Prechter, *Conquer the Crash*

interchangeable, making it more convenient than gold or silver as a medium of exchange and facilitator of economic activity. Law was correct in this observation and noted—as Adam Smith would write more than 70 years later in The Wealth of Nations—that a country's wealth should be measured by its output, not by its holdings of precious metals.

Unfortunately, paper money can also be printed at will. More on that later. Though rejected in his native Scotland, Law's ideas would soon find fertile ground on the other side of the English Channel. Upon his death, Louis XIV—the "Sun King"—had left France virtually bankrupt. As it turned out, building Versailles and spending decades at war cost money—a lot of money. About three billion livres, while annual tax revenues were a mere 145 million livres. To put this in perspective, the official U.S. Treasury debt held by the public is $12.8 trillion, and annual tax revenues are $2.8 trillion. That makes the U.S. debt-to-income ratio 4.6 times, while the ratio that Louis XIV bequeathed to his son was an almost unfathomable 21 times!

The interest payments on the debt took up 120 million of the 145 livres in revenues—leaving a mere 25 million to finance the rest of the French government's expenses. Given that annual expenses were 142 million livres, the French crown depended on further access to credit to keep afloat. Suffice it to say that France was a bad credit risk.

Then along came a certain Scotsman.

Because Louis XV was only a young boy when his father died, his uncle Philippe II, the Duc d'Orleans, became the Regent of France. Philippe was in a bind and was willing to try something—anything—to avoid default and collapse. And John Law appeared to have the answer—the creation of new money by a powerful government-chartered bank that would be used to pay off the existing debts. Law would issue stock in the new bank and would use the proceeds of the IPO to buy back government debt. He would also take deposits in coin but issue loans and withdrawals in paper. How is that for quantitative easing?

As Bill Bonner and Addison Wiggin put it in their telling of the story,

> On May 5, 1716, the Banque Generale was founded with 6 million livres in capital and was assured success from the beginning. The Duc declared all taxes must henceforth be paid with notes issued by Law's bank [making Law's notes legal tender]...

> The French national debt at the time would, today, have already been seriously downgraded by Moody's. The billets d'etat—government bonds issued under Louis XIV to pay for his extravagance—were essentially junk bonds...

> The challenge for Law was to buy back the outstanding government debt at the market rate of 21.50 without driving up the price. If investors discovered the government was reclaiming their billets d'etat and that Philippe II could effectively save the royal finances, they would certainly begin asking more than 21.50 per billet. Law solved the problem by offering the bank shares exclusively in exchange for the government bonds.

This initial move only retired a small fraction of the national debt, but Law was far from finished.

Law built trust in his new paper money by making it redeemable for the full par value in gold coin and went so far as to say that any banker unable to meet redemptions on demand "deserved death." His rhetoric worked. The French bought into the scheme hook, line and sinker.

In a truly unusual sign of the times, Law's paper currency actually traded at a *15% premium* to comparable gold coins one year into the scheme. As Law anticipated, the jolt in both the money supply and the velocity of money jump-started the French economy.

France might have prospered had Law stopped there, gradually paying off its debts through a mixture of economic growth and mild inflation, but alas he got cocky. To pay of the country's remaining debts in one grand swoop, Law launched the next phase of his scheme. As Bonner and Wiggin continue,

Law convinced Philippe II to back a trading company with monopoly trading rights over the Mississippi River and France's land claim in Louisiana. Shares in the new company would be offered to the public, and investors would only be allowed to buy them with the remaining billets d'etat on the market [i.e., the existing French Crown junk bonds]. So begins the famed Mississippi Scheme.

Law's new venture, which would come to be known as the Compagnie des Indes, was granted all the possessions of its competitors—the Senegal Company, the China Company, and the French East India company—giving it exclusive French trading rights for the Mississippi River, Louisiana, China, East India, and South America. Law's enterprise also received the sole right to mint royal coins for nine years; it was allowed to act as the royal tax collector for the same amount of time; and it was granted a monopoly on all tobacco trade under French rule...

Immediately after the initial public offering (IPO), applications for shares in the Compagnie des Indes started coming in from all levels of society. So many, in fact, that it took the staff at the bank weeks to sort through all the applications. Traders, merchants, dukes, counts and marquises crowded into the little rue Quincampoix and waited for hours to find out if their subscriptions had been granted. When the final list of subscribers was announced, Law and his awaiting public learned that the shares had been oversubscribed by a factor of six. The immediate result? Shares in the Compagnie des Indes skyrocketed in value.

The Compagnie des Indes—popularly called the Mississippi Company—was France's answer to the Dutch East India Company, but with one critical difference: The Dutch company actually had profitable trading routes. The French trading company had the mosquito-infested bog we today call Louisiana and little else.

The investors that piled in were buying shares in a company without any real business model. How exactly Law intended to make money in Louisiana—a land of tepid swamps, not mountains of gold—was never fully explained. Though we can shake our heads at the silly Frenchmen in retrospect, it is easy to understand their enthusiasm. They were trading in rather junky junk bonds for an exciting opportunity in the New World—an investment that, while ridiculous in retrospect, was no more absurd than buying tech stocks in 1999 or Miami condos in 2005. The "animal spirits" that characterize all financial bubbles were fueled by an exceptionally loose monetary policy, with predictable results.

Impressed with the success of the original paper banknotes, Philippe II decided to expand Law's operation. He renamed the Banque Generale the Banque Royale, made it an official organ of the Crown, and proceeded to expand the money supply by 16 times its previous amount, later increasing it by even more. Suddenly, Ben Bernanke's much maligned "QE2" would seem tame by comparison!

Much of the new money went directly into shares of the Mississippi Company. In a matter of months, the share price rose from 500 livres to 10,000 livres (**see Figure 9.1**), creating a new class of nouveau riche dubbed "millionaires." A cycle developed whereby demand for the Mississippi shares would create demand for new paper currency with which to buy them. And Philippe and Law were only too happy to oblige.

Law's central bank allowed investors to borrow money at low interest rates using their Mississippi shares as collateral. This would be like the Federal Reserve lending you money directly to buy shares of a new, unproven technology start-up company using your existing shares of the company as collateral. This set up something of a self-contained Ponzi scheme. (The excesses in the mortgage markets during the mid-2000s, in which government-sponsored entities provided almost unlimited capital for additional mortgage loans on increasingly generous terms shows that, as the French say, "Plus ça change, plus c'est la même chose." The more things change, the more they stay the same.)

In the later stages of the scheme, the Banque and Mississippi Company were effectively merged and there was no discernable difference between bank notes, Mississippi shares, and the old government debt. The system evolved from a paper system backed by a gold standard to paper system backed by Mississippi shares, which were in turn "backed" by land in Louisiana. (How the currency would be redeemed for land was, again, never really explained.)

The entire scheme began to unravel when Law attempted to gently deflate the bubble, which had already led to hyperinflation throughout the French economy and which had spread to neighboring England as well. The surge in liquidity created by Law's scheme spilled across the English Channel and helped to inflate the South Sea Bubble, which had its own excesses nearly as legendary as those of France.

When investors attempted to redeem their banknotes for gold, it quickly became obvious that there was not enough metal coinage to back the banknotes in circulation. The bank stopped payment on its notes, and Law was forced to flee the country in disgrace. Shares in the Mississippi Company fell all the way back to their issue price, destroying both the newly rich and the established order alike.

The only thing more painful than hyperinflation is the inevitable deflation that follows. When the credit markets seized up, the supply and velocity of money plummeted as desperate Frenchmen scurried to dump their worthless banknotes and shares. France and her middle and upper classes were ruined, and the monarchy was discredited—setting the stage for the bloody French Revolution a generation later. The French developed a strong distaste for banking and capital markets that arguably lingers to this day. The debacle set back the development of modern capitalism in France by decades.

As for the investors, they endured a bear market that would make modern investors shudder. Take a look at Figure 9.2. Though reliable French stock market data is hard to come by, we can use British data as a proxy. As I mentioned before, London had a market bubble of its own—the South Sea Bubble—that coincided with the Mississippi Bubble. This is the sharp spike you see around the year 1720.

What followed was 70 years of bear market conditions. Stocks did not meaningfully rise again until the 1790s. So much for "stocks for the long run" or "buy-and-hold" investing!

The Mississippi Bubble in Perspective

I have always believed that history—and particularly economic and market history—tends to follow long cycles. For this reason I find a lot of value in reading economic history books. One well-researched economic history book can add clarity that can get lost in the daily barrage of newspaper and magazine articles. Once in a while, a real gem that is both insightful and eminently readable rises to the top. I would put Niall Ferguson's recent book in that category. *The Ascent of Money: A Financial History of the World* is exactly what it claims to be. It is a comprehensive history of the development and rise of the financial industry and its impact on the world. As Ferguson writes,

> *Behind each great historical phenomenon there lies a financial secret, and this book sets out to illuminate the most important of these. For example, the Renaissance created such a boom in the market for art and architecture because Italian bankers like the Medici made fortunes by applying Oriental mathematics to money [starting as far back as 1202 with the publication of Fibonacci's Liber Abaci and climaxing in the high Renaissance of the 1500s]. The Dutch Republic prevailed over the Habsburg Empire because having the world's first modern stock market was financially preferable to having the world's biggest silver mine [in the Dutch independence wars from 1568-1648]. The problems of the French monarchy could not be resolved without a revolution because a convicted Scots murderer had wrecked the French financial system by unleashing the first stock market bubble and bust [in 1719-1720]. It was Nathan Rothschild [and his bond trading] as much as the Duke of Wellington who defeated Napoleon at Waterloo [in 1815].*

Financial history is a long recurring cycle in which power shifts back and forth from creditors to debtors. The same can be said of the cyclical nature of the reputation of financiers, a.k.a. bankers. During boom times, they are viewed as providential stewards of prosperity, but during busts they are vilified and hunted down.

In his study of financial bubbles over the centuries, Ferguson identifies five typical stages:

> **Displacement:** *Some change in economic circumstances creates new and profitable opportunities for certain companies.*
>
> **Euphoria or overtrading:** *A feedback process sets in whereby rising expected profits lead to rapid growth in share prices.*
>
> **Mania or bubble:** *The prospect of easy capital gains attracts first-time investors and swindlers eager to bilk them of their money.*
>
> **Distress:** *The insiders discern that expected profits cannot possibly justify the now exorbitant price of the shares and begin to take profits by selling.*
>
> **Revulsion or discredit:** *As share prices fall, the outsiders all stampede for the exits, causing the bubble to burst altogether.*

Though the focus of Ferguson's analysis was the stock market, the same insights would hold true in the housing and mortgage bubble and burst. "Revulsion" and "discredit" are words that aptly describe public views of investment real estate, mortgage lending and the financial sector in general.

Of course, it could be worse. The boom and subsequent bust that has caused so much misery today is nothing compared to aftermath of the Mississippi debacle.

The crash of the Mississippi bubble brought with it a period of prolonged deflationary weakness, as have all major bubbles in history. As a recent example, in the wake of the Internet bubble and bust we did not see large-scale consumer or producer price deflation, but we did see severe deflation in the areas most directly affected, namely technology and telecom hardware. As Thomas Friedman explained in The World is Flat, the massive price deflation in fiber optic communications is what made the boom in Indian outsourcing and high-tech globalization possible.

It is during the long, post-boom cooling period in which the excesses of the prior boom are worked off. And this is the most important point that we would take from Ferguson's book. Niall Ferguson is one of the few economic commentators who shares my view that deflation, not inflation, will be the threat going forward—and specifically, asset deflation (as opposed to consumer price deflation). I do expect the Fed to try their damnedest to create inflation, and they will probably be successful, at least for a while, in some pockets of the commodities markets. In these cases, commodities cost more because the dollar depreciates and commodity prices rise. However asset inflation in big ticket items like real estate will prove dangerously elusive, and that is a big problem for homeowners and investors.

So, what does this mean for our current situation? While I would expect continued deflation in the housing sector for years to come, there will likely be some residual benefits. The oversupply of housing will mean that young families in the years ahead will get phenomenal bargains on their homes, values perhaps not enjoyed in a generation. In fact, deflation is a common thread throughout all past end-of-cycle economic busts. Without deflation at some point, the next generation could simply not afford to live. Although painful, it is a necessary evil.

But to repeat, I would view any increase in the inflation rate in the months ahead as being temporary noise. As the history of bubbles has proven, it is deflation that accompanies a bust, not inflation. And the broader the scope of the bubble, the more likely it is that deflation spreads to consumer prices in general. The government can and will fight it tooth and nail, but there is little they will be able to do about it in the end.

What lessons can we learn from this? One point on which nearly all market historians would agree is that the bigger the bubble, the bigger the bust that follows. Bubbles almost always return to the level at which they started. This was the case in the Mississippi Scheme— the share price rose from 500 livres to over 10,000 livres before collapsing back to 500—and it will likely be the case in the American real estate markets most affected by the bubble of the mid-2000s. It's not different this time.

Perhaps the most important lesson would be that credit-fueled bubbles always end badly. This was certainly the case with the spectacular collapse of the Japanese "miracle economy" at the beginning of the 1990s and the U.S. housing bubble—which led to the destruction of the banking system.

It is popular these days to lay all blame at the feet of the Fed for keeping interest rates artificially low. In the U.S. housing bubble, this is not really accurate or fair. The Fed played its part, of course, but so did irresponsible bankers, mortgage brokers, real estate agents, and even the home buyers themselves. As the Baby Boomers began to age and cut back their spending on housing in the mid-2000s, the financiers came up with more and more creative ways to extend credit to make up for the loss of natural consumer demand. If fewer people were interested in buying, better give those who were interested more credit to make up the difference. During boom times, everyone becomes punch drunk with self-indulgence if not outright greed, believing this time is different. What we know is, it most certainly was not!

The Fed's actions in the aftermath of the bust generated the most controversy. The Fed is now the biggest holder of U.S. Treasury debt. The Fed has always engaged in "open market operations," buying and selling U.S. government securities in an attempt to regulate the money supply. But this has evolved from a purely monetary objective to becoming a de facto funding mechanism for the U.S. government. The government is effectively printing money at the Fed in order to lend it to itself when the Fed uses that money to buy bonds that it will likely never sell. Though not quite as egregious as the Mississippi Scheme, whereby money was printed to buy inflated shares, there are obvious parallels.

Regardless, we should learn from the lessons of history. Quantitative easing is dangerous and does not "fix" a bad economy. It does, however, generally lead to destabilizing asset bubbles. The quantitative easing following the "dot com" bust helped to create the conditions that made the housing and mortgage bubble possible. And today, rather than fix the root causes of the financial crises, yet another bubble is being formed, and you had better know how to play with bubbles.

CHAPTER 10:

HEALTH CARE, INSURANCE AND TAXES

Taxes are always one of the biggest points of contention no matter where you live. On the one hand I like to say that I hope I pay a lot of taxes because it means that I made a lot of money. On the other hand, if you happen to live in and work in the high-tax state of California, then it takes on a whole new meaning. Currently, the top bracket is about 57% and rising. That's frickin ridiculous! Don't they realize that every dollar we spend in taxes is a dollar we cannot spend on ourselves, so we expect our government to spend those dollars wisely.

With this in mind, I am reminded of a very insightful quote from Leon Levy, a legendary investor and one of the founders of the Oppenheimer family of mutual funds: "Tax codes reflect the values of a society."

When Levy wrote this in his book The Mind of Wall Street , he used the word "reflect," but what he should have said is "shape." Rightly or wrongly, there are few methods of persuasion (or coercion) as effective as the tax code. As Levy continues,

> It is no accident that the French produce great wine. The French tax code used to favor the producers of the spectacular first-growth wines, who were taxed at a lower rate than those who made vin ordinaire. The tax code thus gave producers an incentive to improve their wines. I have thought about the myriad ways in which money flows toward tax incentives and away from high taxes and have concluded that taxes play a profound role in shaping history. Give officials control of the tax code and they can change society, either deliberately through the wise use of incentives or, more commonly, inadvertently through a

misunderstanding of how people react to taxes.[20]

Well said, Mr. Levy. Think about this for a minute. In how many ways has tax policy shifted the behavior of companies and individuals in the United States?

An obvious example is the mortgage interest deduction, which made owning a home more affordable but which also encouraged Americans to buy bigger and more expensive homes than they otherwise might have. It also nudged marginal homebuyers of questionable credit quality into buying homes using subprime mortgages—and we know how that turned out. The tax deduction was "successful" in that it accomplished the government goal of increasing home ownership. Of course, it's a matter of debate as to whether this was a worthwhile policy, particularly after the mortgage meltdown of 2007-2009.

The government has somewhat mixed motives when it comes to taxing vices. In the late 1910s, one of the biggest arguments against

Figure 10.1: Health Spending as % of GDP

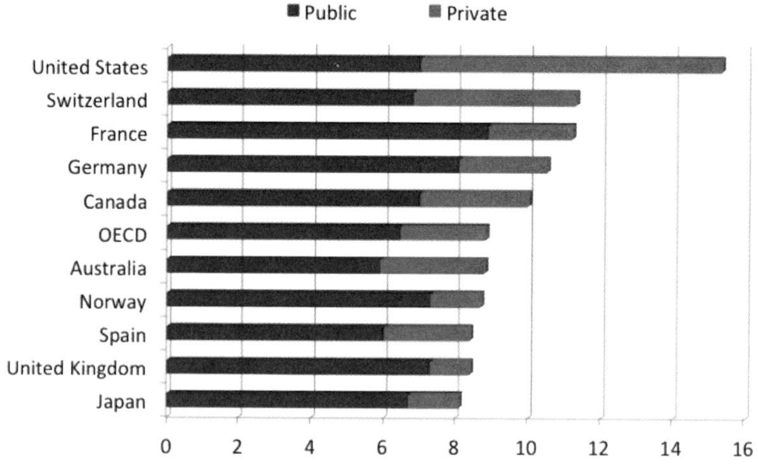

Source: Society at a Glance: OECD Social Indicators

national prohibition of alcohol was not personal freedom; it was the loss of tax revenue for the Federal government. The progressives who campaigned for 18th amendment—which gave us prohibition—first had to campaign for the 16th amendment—which gave us the income tax and the IRS. Naturally, during the pits of the Great Depression, when income tax receipts were plummeting, President Roosevelt abandoned his previous "dry" views and became a proponent of legalizing alcohol again.

Similarly, while the state governments publically have to condemn the tobacco companies, they would be devastated if Americans actually quit smoking. The loss of tax revenue would be a disaster, especially during this period of falling income and property tax receipts. So, they continue their little song and dance—continuing to tax and regulate the industry while making sure that they don't kill the goose that lays all of those golden eggs.

In a sign of true desperation during the crisis in 2008, the governor of New York proposed a punishing tax on fattening food and drink. As

Figure 10.2 Total Health Spending

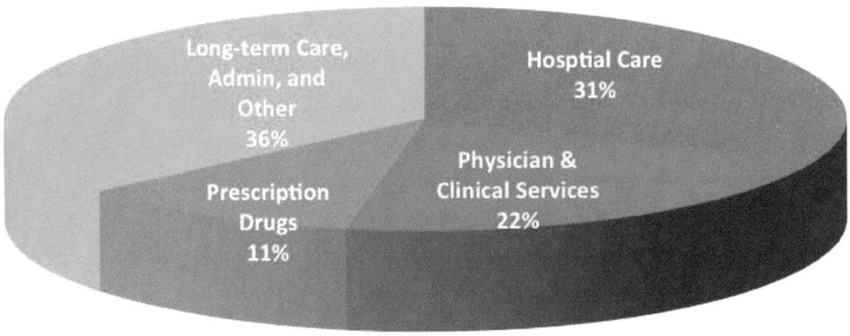

Source: "Improving Healthcare: A Dose of Competition."

Clyde Haberman described it in the *New York Times*:

> *With his tax proposals this week, Gov. David A. Paterson joined a long line of New York leaders who have counted on self-wounding, even self-destructive behavior to help them dig out of budget holes. Mr. Paterson called for a huge tax, 18 percent, on sugary sodas and juice drinks. It's a public health measure, his lieutenants said—you know, to counter the obesity epidemic.*
>
> *Sure. The $404 million tax haul that the governor expects next year is merely incidental, right?*[21]

If Mr. Haberman has a touch of cynicism in his writing, he is certainly entitled to it. New Yorkers have seen this before, always with the stated intent of preserving public health. But, as Mr. Haberman continues, "The last thing that government wants is for everyone, right this minute, to stop smoking, boozing, gambling and downing those nutritionally empty supersweet sodas. Too much money is at stake."

As if the fat tax was not bad enough, the governor also proposed 88 assorted sales or use tax hikes, most notably on clothes, taxis, movie tickets, and "digitally delivered entertainment services" such as iTunes. Of course, these hikes probably will have unintended consequences, such as a transfer of business to out-of-state "e-tailers" like Amazon.com that are not subject to sales taxes. This will hurt New York's store owners. The hikes also are likely to lead to increased smuggling and, in the case of the iTunes tax, even greater levels of Internet piracy.

In the business world, consider the case of corporate dividends. There is a considerable amount of academic literature discussing the "principle-agent" problem of corporate management. Managers do not always act in the best interests of shareholders; they often have their own agendas, driven perhaps by ego and the desire to "build empires" (and ultimately, to secure large paychecks for themselves). The result is that they often waste a large amount of investor capital on suboptimal projects.

The dividend is an excellent tool to keep managements in line. Paying out cold, hard cash to investors limits managers' ability to use aggressive accounting to make themselves look better; they must have the actual cash to back it up. Plus, by taking excess cash out of the hands of ambitious CEOs, you force them to do more with less, encouraging efficiency and better use of investor capital.

So, if dividends are so great, why do most companies pay out such a small percentage of their earnings? As you might guess, the answer is taxes. The double taxation of dividends makes it woefully tax-inefficient to pay investors in cash. So instead, companies often use their earnings to make "investments" of questionable value or in buying back their own shares. In theory, share buybacks are equivalent to dividends in delivering shareholder value; in practice, managements tend to be horrible market timers, buying their own shares when prices are expensive at bull market tops and failing to buy when stocks are cheap at bear market bottoms— yet another way for them to burn investor capital.

Death and Taxes

Perhaps no tax is more controversial than the "death tax." The estate tax has a long and colorful history and is actually one of the oldest taxes in America; it has been used at varying times and in varying forms since colonial times. In the Old World, its use can be traced all the way to the Egyptian pharaohs in 700 BC. Likewise, Caesar Augustus imposed an estate tax in ancient Rome (which is ironic, because Augustus himself rose to power with the inheritance he received from the slain Julius Caesar, in what could be the most famous contested probate case in history). The Heritage Foundation published a brief history of the estate tax in its January 2004 issue of the Backgrounder.[22] I will summarize their history in the paragraphs below.

The first U.S. experiment with an estate tax was the 1797 Stamp Act, used to pay off debts from the undeclared war with France. The act required a federal stamp on all wills in probate. It was repealed in 1804, and Americans were spared the estate tax until the Civil War, when the Tax Act of 1862 used an inheritance tax to raise funds for the federal army. Lincoln's inheritance tax was repealed in 1870 after the dust had settled, and Americans were again spared the estate tax until the next major war.

World War I and the ensuing reduction in world trade cut into the United States' tariff revenues, leading to the passage of the 16th Amendment and the creation of the IRS. The estate tax was brought back yet again and was dramatically increased the following year when the United States entered the war. Alas, it has been with us ever since.

Once the funding needs for the war subsided, policy makers reinvented the estate tax as a form of income redistribution. This was largely popular in a country where wealth was concentrated in the hands of a few well-known families—with names like Rockefeller, Morgan and Ford. However, in the following decades, as the United States progressed into a mass-affluent society, millions of Americans who would at most have considered themselves to be upper middle class have found themselves subject to a rather unpleasant surprise upon the death of a loved one.

Estate tax reform began in the late 1970s, but the reform did not come close to keeping pace with the rise in American wealth. Americans of comparatively average means continued to find themselves subject to the estate tax until former President Bush's tax reforms began to address this.

Just Dying to Save on the Estate Tax

Economics is a study of events at the margin, and Kopczuk and Slemrod's 2001 paper, "Dying to Save Taxes: Evidence from Estate Tax Returns on the Death Elasticity," is a fascinating look at how timing decisions are affected by tax policy.

Kopczuk and Slemrod write:

> There is also evidence that financial considerations affect the timing of decisions that are not generally thought of as being "economic." For example, Sjoquist and Walker (1995) conclude

from an analysis of Census data that the marriage penalty embedded in the U.S. income tax has a significant negative effect on the timing of marriages: as the penalty increases, fewer couples marry in the months of November and December relative to the number of marriages during the first few months of spring in the new year....

[Likewise], Dickert-Conlin and Chandra (1999) find that the timing of births is sensitive to tax incentives. Under the U.S. tax system, the tax benefits of having a child are (fully) realized only if the birth takes place before midnight, January 1. Using a sample of children from the National Longitudinal Survey of Youth, Dickert-Conlin and Chandra find that the probability that a child is born in the last week of December, rather than the first week of January, is positively correlated with tax benefits from so doing; they estimate that increasing the tax benefit by $500 raises the probability of having a child in the last week of December by 26.9 percent.

Surprisingly, a mere $500 tax break encourages a surge of births in the last week of the year. The authors later admit that they cannot say whether this phenomenon is due to natural causes, doctor-induced labor, or even ex post facto falsification of the birth records to get the tax benefit. Kopczuk and Slemrod continue:

If birth, why not death? ... There is a substantial body of evidence corroborating this phenomenon in other contexts. Phillips and King (1988) report that, among Jews, the number of deaths was lower than expected in the week before Passover and higher than expected in the week after; the pattern was most pronounced in years when the holiday fell on a weekend, when it is most likely to be celebrated by the largest number of people. Phillips and Smith (1990) find that mortality among Chinese dips by 35.1% in the week before the Harvest Moon festival and peaks by the same amount in the week after. Anson and Anson (1997) find a similar effect related to the timing of Ramadan for Muslims living in Israel, and note that the effect was larger for women than for men, reflecting their different roles in the celebration of the holy day rites.

Kopczuk and Slemrod go on to say that "...a non-zero death elasticity is consistent with the notion of a bequest motive." In other words, if the timing of death is somewhat flexible, people will subtly alter the timing of their death to avoid the estate tax and thus to pass on more money to their heirs. Putting some numbers behind this, the authors found that, among those dying within two weeks before or after a change in the estate tax rate, a $10,000 potential tax savings increases the probability of dying before the tax hike by 1.6%. Of course, whether this was altruism on the part of the dying is up for debate.

The authors point out that some decisions, such as whether to remain on life support or to "pull the plug" are made not by the dying person but by their heirs. Thus, it is not clear whether the authors' findings were indicative of altruism on the part of the dying or cold manipulation on the part of would-be beneficiaries. At any rate, the data makes it obvious that tax policy does indeed have a predictable effect on human behavior, be it an altruistic or calloused one. Just a little something for our lawmakers to keep in mind as they prepare to negotiate the future direction of the estate tax!

One of the hallmarks of George W. Bush's fiscal program was the elimination of the estate tax and a reduction in taxes in general. But it can always come back in a hurry. It's easier politically to raise taxes on "rich" heirs than on the working man.

Bottom line: Even if your net worth currently exempts you from the estate tax, understand that these levels and rates can be changed at the pleasure of Congress at any time. Hope for the best, but prepare for the worst.

The Health Care Crisis and the Tax Code

While I'm not the biggest fan of ObamaCare, I actually believe that President Obama had good intentions in trying to bring health coverage to those who didn't have it before. But as far as reform goes, it doesn't really fix our problems. It may actually make them worse.

There is a lot of information and misinformation about ObamaCare. Many Americans fear that it was the first step towards a government-controlled, socialized medical system. But what few seem to realize is that we were essentially already there long before ObamaCare, at least by some measures.

The governments of Canada and the United Kingdom—the two countries most often referenced as having "socialized medicine"—spend 7.0% and 7.3% of their respective GDPs on health care. The United States, via Medicare, Medicaid, and other smaller programs, also spends 7% of GDP—and a much larger GDP at that (Figure 10.1). And again, this was before ObamaCare.

Private spending, paid by patients and insurance companies, more than doubles the U.S. total with an additional 8.3%. Combining public and private health spending, health care in the United States

Figure 10.3: Demand for Healthcare

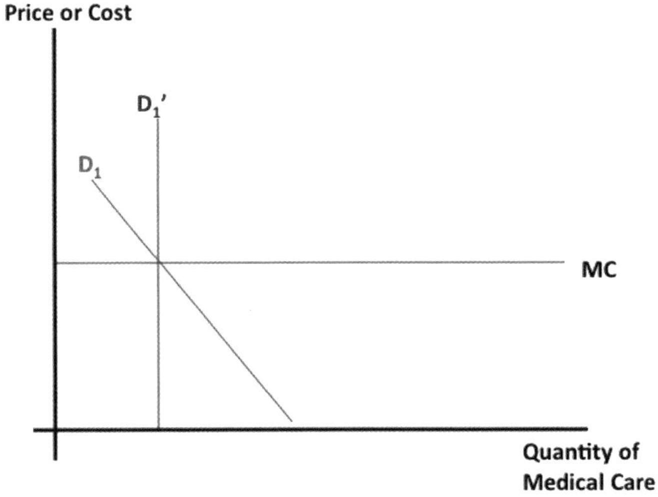

Source: Adapted from Pauly (1968)

is vastly more expensive than anywhere else in the world. And as both statistical measures and casual observation attest, the average American is not any healthier than the average European or Japanese citizen. On the high-end, America is still the world leader in cutting-edge medical techniques. But this does not explain why the prices of basic, standard medical procedures are more expensive here than in other developed nations. It is almost mind-boggling that Japan—despite its eno=rmous population of elderly citizens—spends barely half what the United States does relative to GDP.

With this in mind, let us now consider the state of health care in America. I think we all agree that the system is broken and something has to be done. In my view, ObamaCare was not the answer to our problems. But in defending the status quo, the Republicans are also wrong. The system as it currently stands is absolutely indefensible. There is no justifiable reason for our health system to be roughly twice as expensive as Canada's and the UK's. What exactly are we getting for our money?

Rather than simply protest the Obama plan and threaten to de-fund it, the Republicans should make themselves useful by promoting real reform. President Bush, for his many perceived faults, managed to find a good idea with Health Savings Accounts (HSAs) coupled with high-deductible insurance policies. The former president also proposed making employer-provided insurance "taxable" (though with an offsetting tax credit) in order to make Americans better realize the true cash value of the benefits that they have come to view as "free."

HSAs and tax accounting gimmicks are by no means a comprehensive solution, but they were a step in the right direction. If the Republicans really want to make a positive impact on the country's long-term health (and fiscal health too, for that matter), they will show Americans that their only two choices are not a dysfunctional status quo and an ObamaCare "solution" that will bankrupt the country. They need to propose better alternatives.

As you might have guessed, the tax code is a major contributing factor to the spiraling cost of health care. In my view, the two biggest problems are the "fee for service" compensation model for doctors, which encourages unnecessary testing and procedures, and the high price of malpractice insurance. (These two actually contribute to one another.) The tax code, with its perverse incentives, comes in third.

Essentially, doctors do not get paid for results. They get paid for individual "a la carte" procedures. So, they have every disincentive to attack medical problems in an efficient, holistic way. I do not fault the doctors for this. They didn't create this monster. They, like the rest of us, are just trying to survive the best they can, and in any event doctors do not receive much of the money in question. Take a look at Figure 10.2. Much of the money gets lost in the black hole of administration. The percentage of health spending that actually goes to the doctor is a miniscule 22%.

The problem is that nearly all insurance companies take their pricing model from Medicare guidelines, which encourages the "fee-for-service" model. If Medicare and the broader insurance industry is to remain viable with the aging of the Baby Boomers on the horizon, this must be scrapped. Doctors must be properly incentivized to "fix" medical problems in a more efficient manner. And the reform, if it is to be successful, must start with Medicare.

The second issue, tort reform to reduce the cost of malpractice insurance, ties in very closely with the first. Most Americans would agree that the tort system is out of control. How many of us have watched with disgust (and probably a little envy) as one of our countrymen gets a huge legal settlement far out of proportion to the damage received. Remember the woman who sued McDonalds for millions—and won—after burning herself with hot coffee?

Doctors, fearful of being sued for malpractice, order massive amounts of unnecessary tests and procedures in order to avoid "looking" negligent and leaving themselves open to a malpractice lawsuit. And at the end of the day, the patient doesn't mind (and probably doesn't even notice), because the tab is picked up by their insurance company or the government, and thus "socialized" across the broader population. No one in this chain has any incentive to exercise restraint because, while the costs to society are high, the costs in each case to each person individually are low—generally limited to a nominal co-pay of $20 or so.

This brings us back to my original point about taxes. People and companies, though not "hyper-rational" like the beings described in economics textbooks, generally respond to monetary incentives. Let us consider employer-provided health insurance, which most Americans working for large companies enjoy.

Americans have come to view it as a given that their employer is responsible for providing health insurance while simultaneously viewing it as "socialist" for the government to provide these same services. But why is this?

During the labor shortages of World War II, companies needed to raise wages in order to attract workers, but wartime wage and price controls prevented them from doing so. Health insurance and other benefits became the solution, as they gave companies the ability to effectively increase wages while staying within the letter of the law. As the years rolled by, Congress began to view this arrangement as a social good and created tax incentives to encourage it. Today, your company can write off the value of benefits provided to you, but you do not have to pay income taxes on these benefits. This makes health insurance an extremely tax-efficient way to compensate employees. Unfortunately, it also makes absolutely no economic sense.

Americans view state-provided health insurance as "socialism," but fail to view tax-subsidized insurance using the employer as an intermediary in the same light. Those who defend our "free market" health system are simply wrong. Our system is not "free market" at all, but corporatist. Like the Europeans and Canadians, we too have socialized medicine, only in our system private employers act as middle men.

There are economic consequences for this, of course. American companies have to maintain expensive HR departments to administer benefits, and the insurance premiums paid are real money. This puts them at a disadvantage to foreign competitors who have no such obligation. Consider the pre-bankruptcy General Motors. General

Motors could not compete with Toyota and other rivals because health benefits for current and retired workers added more than $2,000 per car produced. With a $2,000 cost disadvantage, it was only a matter of time until General Motors bled to death. The financial crisis sped up the process, but it would have happened on its own eventually.

So, while I am critical of the employer-provided insurance model, this is not to say I favor socialized medicine. Given the horrid lack of cost control in the Medicare program, I believe that socialized medicine or "socialized medicine lite" via ObamaCare would be an expensive mistake.

Costs can be lowered with the proper incentives—and the tax code can play a significant role in this endeavor. Health costs can be reduced in this country with a reevaluation of the fee-for-service model (starting with Medicare), medical tort reform and an expansion of the consumer-directed health care model, which includes such products as HSAs. But on a more fundamental level, Americans must first come to realize that insurance and medical care are not "free" in any system, be it free-market, corporatist or socialist. We all pay the bill one way or another.

Moral Hazard at the Doctor's Office

No, this section has nothing to do with stem cell research or doctor-assisted suicide. Moral hazard is a very real phenomenon whenever people are shielded from the consequences of their decisions.

Banking is a fine example. Before the Great Depression, there were no protections on your savings other than the good reputation of the bank holding them. A prudent saver in that era would only deposit his or her hard-earned cash in a conservative, safe institution. Unfortunately, the Depression nearly took down the entire banking system, good and bad banks alike. As a result we now have FDIC federal insurance that protects your savings in the event that your bank fails. Most economists view the development of FDIC insurance as a good thing, in that it encourages savers to take their cash out from under the mattress and put it into the system, where it can be used to finance economic growth. Of course, the very same economists would add the caveat that this insurance also has the effect of encouraging excessive risk taking and general carelessness by depositors. After all, why bother investigating the bank's solvency if the government is the one shouldering the risk?

"But," you might protest, "there are costs to the taxpayer. We all pay more in taxes after a federal bailout of a failed bank."

Yes, this is true. But the incremental cost to each individual is small relative to the cost to the system as a whole. No single person has an incentive to act responsibly. This is moral hazard in action. And believe it or not, the situation is even worse when it comes to health care for a number of reasons. First, health care, rightly or wrongly, has a sense of entitlement that other expenses simply do not have. People believe that they have a right to health care, or at the very least, a right to "not die." Not surprisingly, this idea that cost is irrelevant when it comes to saving or improving lives leads to higher costs. After all, it is fine to talk about cutting medical costs, but when it is your family member in the emergency room, those concerns naturally get thrown to the wind. Adding to this is the fact that Medicare is the ultimate payer in many cases, and most people (rightly or wrongly) seem to have no moral qualms with soaking the government. Most patients probably don't even realize that they're doing it.

For perhaps the best analogy to the moral hazard issue, consider Richard Epstein's analogy of teenagers sharing a soda:

> Think of two ways in which a group of 10 teenagers can drink soda at a luncheon counter. One is to get a large pitcher and have 10 thirsty kids each use a straw to take out what he or she wants. The second is to divide the soda into glasses, and assign them one to a person. Let there be 10 pints and each teenager's initial entitlement is one pint either way. The patterns of consumption of the soda will not be the same in these two arrangements. Even if by some miracle each person gets the same amount of soda in the two configurations (which they

won't), we can be 100% confident that the soda will be more rapidly consumed when all 10 teenagers slurp their soft drink from the common pitcher. Consumption rates will slow markedly if each has his or her own glass, for slow sipping now results in greater satisfaction, not a reduction in individual share.[23]

Again, one of the major problems is that the pricing of medical care in this country is either directly or indirectly dictated by Medicare, and Medicare uses an administrative formula, which calculates "appropriate" prices based upon imperfect estimates and fudge factors. Rather than independently calculate prices, private insurers in this country almost universally use Medicare prices as a framework to negotiate payments.[24]

This adds an entirely new element to the moral hazard that plagues the industry. Not only do patients push all responsibility for controlling costs into the hands of insurance companies, but the companies themselves push all of the responsibility into the hands of Medicare! If an insurance company is overcharged for a routine procedure, they can simply raise premiums on the patient's insurance plan and then blame the Medicare pricing scheme for the whole debacle. In the case of company-sponsored plans, an additional level of unaccountability is added since the premiums are paid by the company, not the user of the insurance. Since none of the participants in this little game has any incentive to exercise discipline, it's no shock that excessive and unjustified costs consume as much as 20% of health care spending.[25] With no real responsibility at any point in the chain, it's shocking that our system isn't even more dysfunctional that it is.

One of the best explanations of moral hazard was Mark Pauly's 1968 paper published in the American Economic Review.[26] One point that Mr. Pauly emphasizes is that health insurance offers incentives for patients to over-consume health care. True insurance is designed to protect the policyholder from random, unpredictable and catastrophic events, such as his house being struck by lightning. Insurance is not designed to pay for routine house painting and maintenance. Yet somehow, these same principals have been lost in health insurance. We don't buy health insurance just to protect ourselves from catastrophic diseases, like cancer. We also use it for yearly flu shots and amoxicillin, the medical equivalents of painting and routine maintenance. In practice, it appears that we do not view health insurance as insurance at all, but rather as a medical pre-paid card. More accurately, it could be described as a gift certificate in that we end up buying things that we would never normally buy if we were using our own money. The result is that we over-consume on expenditures that are often frivolous and drive the price higher than it needs to be.

Pauly writes:

> *In order for health insurance to be optimal], the costs of medical care must be random variables. But if such expenses are not completely random, the proposition no longer holds. The quantity of medical care an individual will demand depends on his income and tastes, how ill he is, and the price charged for it. The effect of an insurance which indemnifies against all medical care expenses is to reduce the price charged to the individual at the point of service from the market price to zero.*

Whether or not insurance encourages over-consumption depends on the elasticity of demand for health care. In other words, the elasticity of demand refers to how flexible your purchase decision is. Your demand for food is inflexible—you need it to live. But your demand for, say, beef is very flexible. If it gets too expensive, you can buy chicken instead.

Figure 10.3 illustrates this graphically. Line D_1' is an example of inelastic demand, and as you can see, the amount of health care demanded is the same at all price levels. This is pretty close to reality for life-saving procedures, such as an emergency heart bypass surgery. However, most medical decisions look a lot more like D1. The amount of care demanded decreases as the price increases. There are quite a few noncritical medical procedures you might be willing to forgo were the price high enough. They might be highly desirable, but at some price they are just not worth it. This is where over-consumption and moral hazard comes into play.

As Pauly continues: "Each individual may well recognize that 'excess' use of medical care makes the premium he must pay rise. No individual will be motivated to restrain his own use, however, since the incremental benefit to him for excess use is great, while the additional cost of his use is largely spread over other insurance holders, and so he bears only a tiny fraction of the cost of his use."

This is Epstein's analogy of the teenagers and the pitcher of soda in action. The teenagers end up drinking more soda and drinking it faster with little if any effect on their portion of the lunch tab.

So what's the solution? Abolish all forms of insurance? Doing so would eliminate moral hazard and almost definitely lower prices, but is that really what we want? Most people would lack the financial means to pay for major surgeries and life-saving treatments when they became necessary. Clearly, some kind of insurance is needed. Pauly suggests restricting insurance to cover only catastrophic and relatively random illnesses, like cancer or heart disease. This would be consistent with products such as Health Savings Accounts, which combine a high-deductible insurance policy with a tax-advantaged savings account. Since it is the patient's money and not the insurance company's at stake, patients and doctors alike are likely to use a little more discipline. The result should be lower medical bills, lower premiums, and fewer over-worked doctors.

While any form of insurance is bound to introduce moral hazard into the system, this is not entirely bad. As Clark Havighurst explains, "A degree of moral hazard is a natural concomitant of any arrangement, private or public, that gives people security about their future health care costs. Because such financial security is valuable to people, it is not irrational to incur some higher costs to obtain it."[27] Well said, and I agree completely. We all want security when it comes to our health. The key will be to keep the costs of moral hazard in the health industry to a tolerable minimum, especially given the demands that our system will face as the Boomers age and require ever-increasing amounts of care. For any system to be viable with a looming burden as large as the one we face, there must be a mechanism to make consumers more financially accountable for the services they use. Unfortunately, this means that higher out-of-pocket health care costs for consumers are virtually guaranteed.

This chapter has come a very long way for me to make my original point: Even in a period of stable or slightly falling consumer prices, there can be significant inflation in certain parts of the economy. Health care, unfortunately, is one of them. Some kind of reform—real reform—will eventually happen because it has to. There are practical limits to how much Americans can pay for health care.

Unfortunately, the necessary reforms may still be several years away. America, like most democratic countries, tends to put off difficult decisions until the absolute last moment. It's just one of those quirks of democracy. No matter how idealistic he might be, a politician's primary objective is always to get reelected. For this reason, big reforms are usually only possible when a crisis reaches a boiling point and voters demand them. We're not quite there—yet.

Bottom line: Change will come, eventually. But for the next several years, plan on rising medical prices being the reality. If you currently get your insurance from your employer, expect them to push more of that cost to you.

CHAPTER 11:

THE ART OF MANAGING RISK IN RETIREMENT

In 2008, I bet you thought you weren't taking a lot of risk, that was until you lost 20% to 30% or more! It was then that you probably realized that you were taking more risk than you thought you were or even could be. What made it worse was that you were recently retired or so close you could taste it, and that feeling of security vanished in a heartbeat, or should I say a heart attack!

One of the key lessons in finance is that there is no such thing as a free lunch. If it sounds too good to be true, it probably is.

In the world of investments, we pay for our returns by the risk we take in order to get them. In a bull market, this seems like a pretty good trade-off. Investors made a killing in stocks in the 1990s and a leveraged killing on their homes in the 2000s. Unfortunately, the bill came due in the form of the bear market of 2000-2002 and the housing crash and financial meltdown of 2007-2008. Suddenly, you realized how costly those earlier returns had been, and it turned into a pretty rotten deal!

Investment risk takes a couple different forms. The most benign— but still quite serious—is opportunity cost. This can be thought of as the returns you didn't earn because you invested in something else. For example, if you earned 5% in a bond fund, but the stock fund you didn't buy returned 12%, your opportunity cost is the difference between the two, or 7%.

No one has a crystal ball, of course, and we all suffer from opportunity cost at one time or another. Even the great Warren Buffett, the most successful investor in history, misses out on countless opportunities every year. It's just a part of life that comes

Figure 11.1: The Normal Distribution aka, the "Bell Curve"

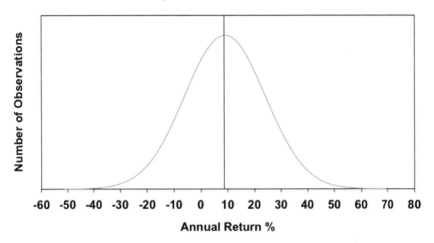

Figure 11.2: Daily Price Changes DJIA 2008

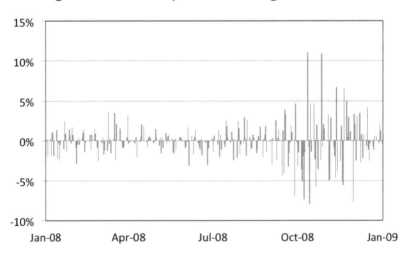

Figure 11.3: Daily Price Changes DJIA 1928-2014

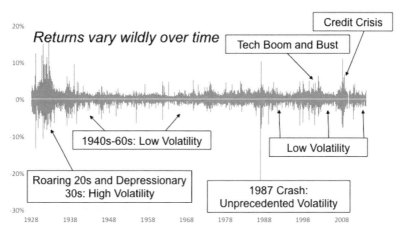

Source: Bloomberg

Figure 11.4: Stock Returns
Normal Distribution Assumed

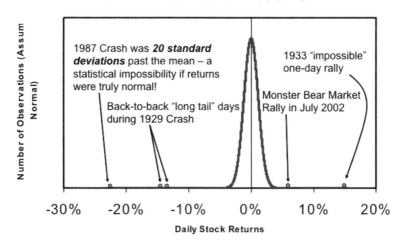

from not having perfect foresight. We're only human, after all.

As investors, we can minimize our opportunity cost by assessing the amount of risk we are prepared to take and allocating our capital to the investments that, given the imperfect information we have to work with, offer the best potential return for the level of risk we're taking.

But more fundamentally—and this goes to the heart of the practice of a good qualified retirement advisor or do it yourself investor—it is best not to fixate on opportunity cost and instead keep the goal in mind. Rather than chase the highest return possible—and put my clients on a financial roller coaster ride that they neither need nor want—I find it makes far more sense to start with the goal and work backwards. If a client starts with $2,000,000 and needs $6,000,000 in the next 15 years to meet his retirement and legacy goals, we can figure out what return is needed to meet that goal and invest accordingly, taking the least amount of risk possible to achieve the necessary return.

Figure 11.5: Leptokurtosis vs. Normal

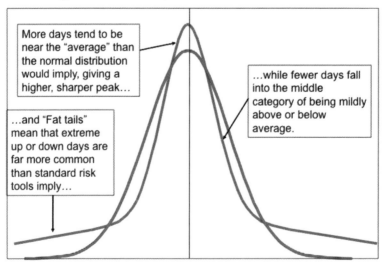

More days tend to be near the "average" than the normal distribution would imply, giving a higher, sharper peak...

...while fewer days fall into the middle category of being mildly above or below average.

...and "Fat tails" mean that extreme up or down days are far more common than standard risk tools imply...

What I have coined (and trademarked) is *"Invest for need, not for greed"™*.

The risk that keeps many in this business awake at night is the risk of outright loss. There are different ways to define this risk. In the investment management industry, it is standard practice to define risk as volatility. This is the basis of modern portfolio theory, which was developed in the 1950s by Harry Markowitz. In the Markowitz model, risk is the degree to which a given investment fluctuates in value. For the math geeks in the room, this is numerically calculated as the "standard deviation of returns." In the decades that followed Markowitz's breakthrough, this concept has been adapted slightly. Some readers might have heard of a stock or mutual fund's "beta." Beta is the degree to which an investment fluctuates relative to its benchmark (usually the S&P 500). An investment with a beta of 1.0 is expected to fluctuate in line with the market. A beta of 1.5 would imply that the investment was 50% more volatile, and a beta of 0.5 would imply that it is half as volatile.

While mathematically elegant, this is not how most people think in the real word. This kind of thinking is also shunned by many "old school" value investors who follow in the footsteps of Benjamin Graham and Warren Buffett. Graham, the father of the investment management profession, considered risk to be the permanent impairment of capital. In other words, risk is the possibility that your investments fall in value and never recover. Investors in General Motors, Bear Stearns, Lehman Brothers, or any of the other companies that went bankrupt during the meltdown would understand this risk all too well.

In this chapter, I want to discuss some of the issues surrounding the popular measures for risk. The goal here is to make a case for a more holistic approach to risk—one that will save your nest egg from the next major financial debacle, whenever it might strike.

When Genius Failed

As Roger Lowenstein recounts in his classic When Genius Failed, the

SURFING THE RETIREMENT TSUNAMI

financial world came very close to ending in 1998, even during one of the strongest bull markets in history. Earlier in the decade, some of the brightest minds in finance—the guys that literally wrote the books that Ivy League finance students study in college—started a hedge fund with the rather boring name of Long-Term Capital Management (LTCM).[28] The group included noted Nobel-Prize-winning scholars such as Myron Scholes (the co-creator of the Black-Scholes option pricing formula) and Robert Merton and Wall Street legends like John Meriwether of Salomon Brothers fame.

The professors and their Wall Street partners sought to take advantage of what they thought were irrational discrepancies in the pricing of similar investments. For example, if French bonds appeared to be cheap relative to German bonds based on their historical relationship, you would buy French bonds and sell German bonds, making money as French bonds rose relative to the German bonds. Of course, the risk involved was that the irrational pricing could go the other way and widen even further, creating a loss. In other words, the market could go from irrational to more irrational.

The professors were not making these trades haphazardly. They used the same financial tools that the industry continues to use today. According to these "normal" tools, the risk of Long-Term Capital Management taking a 10% loss was about 1 in 1,000 years.[29] The risk of a 50% loss was approximately 1 in 10,000,000,000,000,0 00,000,000,000,000 years, or

several billion times the age of our universe. (An event of this magnitude is known as a Black Swan.) Suffice it to say, based on the tools used to measure risk, the fund appeared about as close to "riskless" as you can get.

As you might have already guessed, that's not quite how things worked out in the real world. That "once in a billion years" event happened after just five years. The problem was that the professors' risk models were based on poor assumptions that do not hold up in the real world—the very same assumptions that are used today by many in the investment industry and individual investors. They forgot the golden rule of investing: "The market can stay irrational for longer than you can stay solvent"!

First, they assumed that the distribution of returns for investments or portfolios was "normal," meaning that they followed a bell curve. Second, they expected investments to behave in the future in the same way they had behaved in the recent past.

Nassim Nicholas Taleb, author of the best-selling *Fooled by Randomness and The Black Swan*, refers to this as the "problem of induction." In finance, we base our view of what is possible on what has already happened. Our estimates of returns and volatility are based on the past and then presented as if these "odds" are truly predictable, like a roll of the dice. We know that the odds of rolling any one number on a die are one in six. We don't know what the odds of hitting a certain return in the stock market are. The problem is that the tools used in the industry assume that we do know the odds, and this assumption is dangerous. It lulls investors into a false sense of security about the level of risk they are taking. Related to this is what Taleb calls the "ludic fallacy," or the temptation to view the world of investing like a game of chance. The stock market is often considered to be a form of casino gambling in which one side wins and one side loses. This is certainly a fair comparison. The problem is that the stock market is actually worse than a casino. A casino is a closed system in which you can pre-calculate the odds and the rules do not change halfway through your hand of blackjack. Your chances of receiving an ace will not be 4/52 on one draw and 10/51 on the next. Betting limits do not arbitrarily change at the poker table. The number of red or black spaces on the roulette wheel does not change with every spin. In the real world of finance, all of these things do happen. The stock market is not a roll of the dice, unless you can find a pair of dice that has the ability to change shape after it leaves your hand.

Taleb has dedicated his entire career to debunking this kind of thinking using the example of the Black Swan,[30] which originally came from the work of the philosopher Karl Popper. Popper made the observation that you can observe a million swans that are white and draw the conclusion that all swans are white—but it only takes the sighting of one black swan to prove your theory completely wrong. Europeans believed that all swans were white because they had never observed a black one—until British sailors spotted black swans in Australia during the colonial period. Just because they hadn't seen them before didn't mean they didn't exist.

Taleb took this idea and applied it to modern investing, and I believe his thinking is worth noting. After Taleb popularized the term, "black swan" has come to mean any low probability, high impact event. By nature, they are unpredictable and it is virtually impossible to accurately calculate the odds of one occurring, but when they happen the results are catastrophic. For example, the terror attack of September 11, 2001 was a black swan. No one had ever committed a terrorist act by ramming a plane into a skyscraper before, so it never occurred to Americans to be prepared for it—much less calculate the odds of it happening. The 1987 stock market crash and the 2010 "flash crash," in which the Dow Jones Industrial Average fell almost 10% in a matter of minutes are examples of black swans specifically stemming from the market itself.

Taleb—himself a veteran quantitative trader—takes issue with the modern tendency to quantify risk as a precise number. Risk is no longer a concept; it's a number. This leads to a false sense of security as we rely on a degree of precision that simply isn't there. Think about the subprime mortgage disaster. Banks took far more risk than they should have in lending far too much money on inflated properties to borrowers who often lacked the means to pay. Why? Because their risk models told them it was ok. Similarly, how many "quant" hedge funds blew up during the crisis? The traders traded far more aggressively than would be prudent because their elaborate risk models gave them a false sense of security. Models, of course, are only as good as their inputs. You put garbage in, you get garbage out. It really doesn't matter how elegant the formulas are.

This echoes the words of John Maynard Keynes a generation ago when he said "I'd rather be generally right than precisely wrong." It also ties in with legendary value investor Benjamin Graham who focused on "margin of safety" in his investments and passed that wisdom on to his protégé, Warren Buffett. Buffett jokes that he likes his investments to wear both a belt and suspenders. Because you can never fully know the future or take all unknowns risks into account, you need that all-important margin of safety, which is all too lacking in modern financial theory.

The Unknown Unknowns

"There are known knowns. These are things we know that we know. There are known unknowns. That is to say, there are things that we know we don't know. But there are also unknown unknowns. There are things we don't know we don't know." —Donald Rumsfeld, Former U.S. Secretary of Defense

The above quote is a little convoluted, but it's a valid observation. We plan for things that we know will occur, "known knowns," such as anticipating a curve in the road while driving. Things that we know are possible but we do not know when or if they will occur, such as having a heart attack, are called "known unknowns." Naturally, we don't know when a heart attack might strike, so we buy health insurance to mitigate our risk.

It is the final category, "unknown unknowns," that make life complicated. These are risks that have haven't even imagined.

The September 11 attacks were an example of an unknown unknown, in that no one predicted terrorists would be able to use a hijacked plane, much less several of them, as a missile to take down a building. This is probably the most famous unknown unknown in recent history, but the financial world is full of them. The markets are always finding new ways to take investors by surprise, both on the downside and the upside.

As the 2008-2009 meltdown reminded us, financial risk is not limited to the stock market. In The Black Swan, Mr. Taleb laments the inadequacy of risk management in commercial banks and pokes fun of bankers, generally "dull" middle-aged men who are "clean-shaven and dress in possibly the most comforting and boring manner, in dark suits, white shirts, and red ties."

This conservatism, Taleb insists, is purely superficial:

> *Similarly, think of a bank chairman whose institution makes steady profits over a long time, only to lose everything in a single reversal of fortune... There is no way to gauge the effectiveness of their lending activity by observing it over a day, a week, a month, or... even a century! In the summer of 1982, large American banks lost close to all their past earnings (cumulatively), about everything they had ever made in the history of American banking—everything. They had been lending to South and Central American countries that all defaulted at the same time— "an event of an exceptional nature." So it took just one summer to figure out that this was a sucker's business and that all their earnings came from a very risky game. All the while the bankers led everyone, especially themselves, into believing they were "conservative."*

> *Just as was the case with the record banking profits in the years leading up to the mortgage meltdown of 2008, the banking profits of the early 1980s were simply cash borrowed from destiny with some random payback time.*

Sadly, it is when we believe that we have been the most successful and that we are being the most conservative that we might in fact be taking the biggest risks!

The Wild and Unexpected

The financial meltdown created quite a few "impossible" events. On Friday, October 24, 2008, the Financial Times reported that "swap spreads turned negative." It would be easy to dismiss this headline as just another bit of media noise except for one little technicality: According to all of the rules of finance, it is a mathematical impossibility. A negative swap spread means that the Treasury yield is higher than that of a swap of a similar maturity. As the "risk free" rate in virtually all financial models, the Treasury should always give the lowest taxable yield without exception. The pricing in the swaps market implies that the private issuers of swaps are somehow less risky than the U.S. government! Of course, this is absurd. All doubts about the fiscal responsibility of the government aside,

162

no private company can ever be less risky than the U.S. government.

With unlimited ability to tax and, if need be, print the needed money, a sovereign government by definition cannot default on debts denominated in its own currency.

Meanwhile, at the same time on the other side of the Atlantic, we found another absurd anomaly. German automaker Volkswagen briefly became the most valuable company in the world! A rush of panicked short covering caused the stock to triple in one day before finally easing to a lower, albeit still grossly overvalued, price. Short sellers of Volkswagen found themselves wiped out... in the middle of an economic contraction that has decimated the auto industry and eventually caused the bankruptcy of General Motors and Chrysler.

Does this sound like a rational or efficient market to you? Yeah, me neither. Yet all mainstream investment tools make the assumption that the markets are a model of rationality.

The Nuts and Bolts of Modern Finance

Sometimes it can be useful to step back and ask an obvious question? Why exactly do we invest? The answer, of course, is to make money. When we invest, we expect to earn a return on our investment. If we put our money in the bank, we expect to earn interest, even if the rate is a little on the low side. We also know, with absolutely certainly, what our returns will be on our bank savings. The same is not true of stock market investments, of course. In the stock markets, you can experience a wide spectrum of returns, including some years with substantial losses—like 2008—or extraordinary gains—like 2009. Our reward for putting our capital at risk in the stock market—our "risk premium" in financial parlance—is the possibility of larger returns than would be earned on "risk free" alternatives, like Treasury bonds or a CD at the bank.

This is where it starts to get messy. How do you estimate what stock returns will be? Well, that's the problem. There is no reliable way to estimate future stock returns. So, standard industry practice is to simply take the average of past returns and use that as an estimate for the future. Professor Jeremy Siegel—whom I mentioned in previous chapters—calculated that over history stocks have returned 9%, before taking into account the effects of inflation. However, we also

know that it is uncommon for the large-company stock index to ever actually earn 9% (only twice in the last 80 years has the S&P 500 index been within 1% of this number). Given that stocks rarely return their "expected" return, we instead estimate the likelihood that stock returns will fall within a certain range around our "expected" 9%. Mainstream investment analysis assumes that returns are distributed in what is called a normal distribution—or bell curve. Figure 11.1 shows a normal distribution for annual stock market returns.

A normal distribution assumes that all of the data points are independent (like the idea that sequential rolls of dice are unrelated to each other) and that the observations are distributed identically. In other words, a bad year does not cause the next year to be good, and a good year does not cause the next year also to be good. Again, using the dice analogy, rolling snake eyes on your first roll does not make it any more likely that your next roll will be double sixes.

Of course, when it comes to investing, we know this is not true. Returns are dependent on prior returns, and anyone familiar with the markets knows that they can go through days, weeks, or even months of extreme turbulence—think 2008—followed by long stretches of relative calm.

Figure 11.2 plots the daily returns of the Dow Jones Industrial Average in 2008. The chart should quickly dispel any belief that returns are independent or identically distributed. Taking a longer view, Figure 11.3 plots daily returns from October 1928 to the present. For most of the history of the US stock market, daily volatility has been relatively small and uniform with only a few larger-than-usual moves, as a normal distribution would predict. However, the late 1920s and the 1930s tell a very different story. In those years, daily moves of more than 10% were pretty common. One data point truly stands out: October 19, 1987, the day the Dow fell 23%.

If investment returns really do follow a normal distribution pattern, then the 1987 crash never should have happened—never, not once in a billion years. The problem is that the stock market is full of "once every billion years" days, even though we have only about 80 to 100 years' worth of reliable data. So, what does that actually mean? Suffice it to say that mainstream investment tools are flawed.

To illustrate how not-normal the stock market really is, I plotted the returns from **Figure 10.3** on the normal distribution to see where they fall (**Figure 11.4**).

As you can see, Figure 11.4 is full of observations in the extreme ends of the bell curve. This type of chart is referred to as a normal distribution with "fat tails," which means that extreme moves are far more common than the financial services industry assumes

Figure 11.5 illustrates the difference between a normal distribution and a fat-tailed distribution, more technically called "leptokurtic." Leptokurtic distributions can vary in terms of the fatness of the tails and the pointedness of the peak. The actual distribution of historical stock returns is a little less exaggerated than **Figure 10.5** would suggest, but the point is to show you that there is a clear difference between the models and reality.

Dealing with Risk and Return

No one complains about making too much money. While saving too much can impact your current standard of living, it is not what we would think of as a problem. The other end of the spectrum, saving too little, is all too common. When it comes to retirement, most of us are trying to figure out how to plan for the unknowable, which is how long we will live and how much it will cost. Once we have rough estimates of these two things, which is hard enough, then comes the second daunting task: determining how much to save. Simply put, the amount we need to save is based on how much we think we will need, how many years we can invest, and how much we think we will earn on our investment. It takes a lot of homework to make several of these estimates, but the last one, how much we will earn, is anybody's guess. Not only do extreme returns occur more frequently than we think, but they have long-lasting implications for our portfolio decisions. For this reason, income is a particularly valuable part of a portfolio. Income in the form of dividends and interest is real income, not ephemeral capital gains, hence the old market maxim "A bird in hand is worth two in the bush." Or as Tom Cruise and Cuba Gooding, Jr. screamed in Jerry Maguire, "Show me the money!"

It also pays to stay tactical. If you're willing to trade more actively, you can take risk on or off the table as your needs warrant. This is the approach I take with most of my equity portfolios.

Lessons Not Learned During the Crisis

People underestimate the power of the market to induce amnesia in the masses. The worst financial meltdown in 100 years is a recent painful memory, yet investors are already back to business as usual. I have found that people's memory is about 18 months. 2008 was excruciatingly painful for everyone. However, I probably have a better memory of it because I was on the front lines and I can remember the actual mental and physical toll. Getting calls from clients for comfort, reporters for quotes and cable news outlets for analysis, sometimes as many as four a day. The pain is fresh. However, in general, it appears that we are hard wired to not learn our lessons. With that said, here is James Montier's Top Ten List of lessons not learned (all quotes are directly from Montier's white paper):[31]

Lesson 1: Markets aren't efficient.

"As I have observed previously, the Efficient Market Hypothesis (EMH) is the financial equivalent of Monty Python's Dead Parrot. No matter how many times you point out that it is dead, believers insist it is just resting."

Montier is on to something here. While many in the profession have come to accept the obvious—that markets are neither efficient nor rational—the academic establishment has been reluctant to let it go. It's understandable; despite the theory's failings, there is more than 50 years of accumulated research, and a repudiation of the theory would mean that some of the leading academics spent their entire careers figuratively chasing their tails.

Lesson 2: Relative performance is a dangerous game.

The key question in the investment management industry is not, "How much money did you make me?" or "How much money did you save me by being out of the market?" but rather "Did you beat the market?"

But does this kind of thinking really make sense? Does it make sense to benchmark every portfolio to the S&P 500 or a similar index? Doesn't this encourage the manager to take excessive risk and then blame "the market" if it doesn't pan out?

Relative performance creates perverse incentives for investment managers. As Montier writes, "Put in our terms, many (if not most) investment managers are more worried about career risk (losing your job) or business risk (losing funds under management) than they are about doing the right thing!"

Montier knows a little something about that. His firm, GMO, lost a good deal of its assets because Jeremy Grantham steadfastly refused to buy tech stocks during the dot com craze of the late 1990s. Grantham was ultimately proven right, and the investors that stuck with him avoided the bear market of 2000-2002 and made great money in years that followed. But in the interim, Grantham's firm suffered for doing the right thing.

Lesson 3: The time is never different.

I dedicated an entire chapter to this concept, but frankly, Montier explains it better than I do:

> *Contrary to the protestations of the likes of Greenspan, Bernanke, and Brown, bubbles can be diagnosed before they burst; they are not black swans. The black swan defense is*

nothing more than an attempt to abdicate responsibility. A good working knowledge of the history of bubbles can help preserve your capital. Ben Graham argued that an investor should "have an adequate idea of stock market history, in terms, particularly, of the major fluctuations. With this background he may be in a position to form some worthwhile judgment of the attractiveness or dangers... of the market." Nowhere is an appreciation of history more important than in the understanding of bubbles.

Well said, Mr. Montier.

Lesson 4: Valuation matters.

Buy low and sell high. It sounds simple, doesn't it? Yet few seem to get this right. Instead, investors—both retail and professional—tend to chase growth and pay too much for it. Whether it's stocks, Miami condos, or gold, investors tend to pile in only after an asset has had a good run. Alas, humans are herd animals. Montier's comments here are quite insightful:

At its simplest, value investing tells us to buy when assets are cheap and to avoid purchasing expensive assets. This simple statement seems so self-evident that it is hardly worth saying. Yet repeatedly I've come across investors willing to undergo mental contortions to avoid the valuation reality... Buying when markets are cheap generates significantly better returns than buying when markets are expensive. Of course, the flip side is that one must be prepared to not be fully invested when the returns implied by equity pricing are exceptionally unattractive.

Lesson 5: Wait for the fat pitch.

"Warren Buffett often speaks of the importance of waiting for the fat pitch—that perfect moment when patience is rewarded as the ball meets the sweet spot. However, most investors seem unable to wait, forcing themselves into action at every available opportunity, swinging at every pitch, as it were."

There is something about baseball that makes it uniquely suited for investment metaphors, and the idea of waiting for the fat pitch is certainly one of them. Warren Buffett made out like a bandit during the meltdown because he had cash at his disposal at a time when everyone wanted and needed cash. He made emergency loans to Goldman Sachs and General Electric at what amounted to pawnshop rates of interest because he waited for the fat pitch. The lesson here: Don't waste your strikes swinging at subpar investments!

Lesson 6: Sentiment matters.

"Investor returns are not only affected by valuation. Sentiment also plays a part. It is a cliché that markets are driven by fear and greed, but it is also disturbingly close to the truth. Sentiment swings like a pendulum, from irrational exuberance to the depths of despair."

Sometimes investing in the market can seem like carrying on a conversation with a crazy person. Benjamin Graham joked about this as far back as the 1930s, personifying the stock market as "Mr. Market," a wildly manic depressive gentleman who offers to sell his inventory at a bargain price one day and a ridiculously inflated price the next.

Lesson 7: Leverage can't make a bad investment good, but it can make a good investment bad!

Never were truer words spoken. The real tragedy of the 2008 meltdown is that the basic business model—pooling and securitizing mortgage loans—is actually quite good. But when you added in irresponsible lending practices and then turbocharged the entire thing with insane amounts of leverage... well, it became a ticking time bomb. This is what blew up Long-Term Capital Management a decade before. Had the professors not been leveraged 40-to-1, they could have waited out the period of volatility. They'd probably still be in business. Unfortunately, debt is like crack cocaine for the investment industry, and it's an almost impossible addiction to break. As Montier writes,

Leverage is a dangerous beast. It can't ever turn a bad

investment good, but it can turn a good investment bad. Simply piling leverage onto an investment with a small return doesn't transform it into a good idea. Leverage has a darker side from a value perspective as well: it has the potential to turn a good investment into a bad one! Leverage can limit your staying power, and transform a temporary impairment (i.e., price volatility) into a permanent impairment of capital.

Lesson 8: Over-quantification hides real risk.

This is something I discussed earlier in this chapter. At its root, investing is not complicated. Warren Buffett—the best in the business—went years without having even a single computer in his office. This is not to say it's easy. If it were, we would all be Warren Buffett!

The current obsession with quantifying everything does make the business unnecessarily complicated, however, and it distorts the idea of what risk really is—a concept, not a precise number. Montier does a good job of explaining this:

> *Finance has turned the art of transforming the simple into the perplexing into an industry. Nowhere (at least outside of academia) is overly complex structure and elegant (but not robust) mathematics so beloved. The reason for this obsession with needless complexity is clear: it is far easier to charge higher fees for things that sound complex.*

Two of my investing heroes were cognizant of the dangers posed by elegant mathematics. Ben Graham wrote: "Mathematics is ordinarily considered as producing precise and dependable results; but in the stock market the more elaborate and abstruse the mathematics the more uncertain and speculative are the conclusions we draw there from... Whenever calculus is brought in, or higher algebra, you could take it as a warning that the operator was trying to substitute theory for experience, and usually also to give to speculation the deceptive guise of investment."

The key insight here is the substituting of theory for experience.

Theory is important, of course. It's what helps us understand what is happening in the markets. But you have to keep a sense of perspective, and it's pretty obvious that this was lost in the run-up to the 2008 meltdown.

Lesson 9: Macro matters.

Some readers might remember the old *Miller Lite* commercials in which the world was divided in two camps—those that believed the beer tasted great and those that believed it was less filling. The closest thing in the world of investments to this kind of thinking would be the debate over which investment approach is better: top-down, or bottom-up.

In a nutshell, the "top-down" approach resembles a funnel. This is the approach I generally take in my practice. I look at the overall economy and market conditions and make a judgment first on the market as a whole. I ask myself, "Do I even want to be in stocks based on economic conditions?" From there I will identify what areas or sectors will benefit in the current environment. On down the line, I focus on how much goes towards growth and how much towards value and so on until I find the best individual investments. This is the basis for my *Top-Down Tactical*™ investment strategy, which is the foundation of my firm's success.

In contrast, a "bottom-up" investor ignores the "noise" of current economic conditions and instead looks for investments that are attractively priced. This is how most forms of traditional value investing work, and under some market conditions it is safe to ignore the macro. But this would have been a disaster in the recent crisis. As Montier explains,

Ignoring the top-down can be extraordinarily expensive. The credit bust has been a perfect example of why understanding the top-down can benefit and inform the bottom-up. The last 12 months have been unusual for value investors as two clear camps emerged from their normally more homogenous whole. A schism over financials has split value investors into two diametrically opposed groups…

Essentially, the difference between these two camps comes down to an appreciation of the importance of the bursting of the credit bubble. Those who understood the impact of the bursting of such a bubble didn't go near financials. Those who focused more (and in some cases exclusively) on the bottom-up just saw cheapness, but missed the value trap arising from a bursting credit bubble. It often pays to remember the wise words of Jean-Marie Eveillard.

"Sometimes, what matters is not so much how low the odds are that circumstances would turn quite negative, what matters more is what the consequences would be if that happens." In terms of finance jargon, expected payoff has two components: expected return and probability. While the probability may be small, a truly appalling expected return can still result in a negative payoff.

Neither top-down nor bottom-up has a monopoly on insight. We should learn to integrate their dual perspectives.

Well said. In this business, one approach does not work best at all times. Focusing just on one school of thought is mental laziness, and we are not likely to be successful as investors when we go down that road.

Lesson 10: Look for sources of cheap insurance.

"The final lesson that we should take from the 2008-09 experience is that insurance is often a neglected asset when it comes to investing. The cash flows associated with insurance often seem unappealing in a world when many seem to prefer 'blow up' (small gain, small gain… big loss) to 'bleed out' (small loss, small loss… big gain)."

It was this line of thinking that prompted me to create our TDT™ Protected Dividend Strategy. It combines our Top Down Tactical (TDT™) with a protected dividend approach that captures the dividends and income of high yielding stocks, bonds and preferred stocks, while hedging the principal against a market decline—what I like to call, "Grabbing nickels and dimes in front of the steamroller."

As I mentioned in the introduction, to protect our clients' assets, we use a revolutionary portfolio monitoring and asset-protection system called AssetLock™. We think it's essential for every investor, especially retirees. This system monitors your investments every single day and protects your portfolio from devastating losses by establishing a predetermined downside based on the highest point the portfolio has ever reached, thus locking in gains.

As I previously said, AssetLock™ is a plan B. Plan A is to make money. Plan B is in place in case we go to hell in a hand basket. And in such a case where the AssetLock™ is triggered, we have a plan for systematically re-entering the market by using the Recession Probability Index (RPI). I'm not quite as harsh on the investment management business as James Montier. The optimist in me believes that some of these lessons have indeed been learned, at least by the current generation of financiers. We'll have other bubbles and meltdowns, of course. Eventually, another one is bound to happen, and when they do we emerge a little older and a little wiser. The key for us as investors is to understand risk and to use that understanding to avoid these pitfalls as they come up. No investor misses every bear market or crash, but if you are able to miss even one or two big ones over the course of your investing career, it can make a major difference in your net worth.

CHAPTER 12:

TERROR, WAR AND PREGNANCY

I want to take a little time here to discuss geopolitical risks because this is a topic that generated a lot of headlines in 2014. We had the Russian invasion of Crimea… followed by the Russian invasion of eastern Ukraine. We also had some of the worst violence in years in the Middle East and nasty tensions with Iran.

But while these tend to grab headlines, they are also generally misunderstood by most investors. We tend to fixate on the wrong things. Geopolitics do matter. But I've been in this business long enough to know that the things most people worry about—such as terrorism and small-scale conventional war—tend to have a surprisingly small effect on stock returns over time. A bigger issue is the longer-term reshaping of the world economy, as up-and-coming countries such as China and India gain ground at the expense of established powers like the United States and Europe. Demographics play a big part in these transformations, though the media tends to ignore this because it's too slow-moving to capture their attention.

Terror attacks can have a big effect on the market when they strike. Just think back to September 11, 2001. The New York Stock Exchange remained closed for almost a week, and when it finally reopened, all hell broke loose. The week that followed was one of the worst in the history of the U.S. stock market. But then, a funny thing happened. After finding a bottom in late September, the market turned around and proceeded to rise by almost 30% over the five months that followed.

Similarly, history buffs recall the Wall Street terror attack of 1920 in which an Italian anarchist bombed JP Morgan's headquarters, which sits directly across from the New York Stock Exchange. If you happen to be in New York, walk down Wall Street and take a look. You can still see the pock marks in the side of the building. Needless to say, the attack—which killed 38 and seriously injured another 143—did little to stop the Roaring Twenties and the stock market bubble that characterized that decade. Whether the anarchists liked it or not, the 1920s were one of the best decades in U.S. stock market history. It was the wild excesses of the investors themselves—and not any act of terror or war—that ultimately killed the market in the 1929 Crash.

Israel has spent most of its 60 years of statehood facing legitimate threats to its survival. Despite this, Israel has developed a cutting-edge tech sector and a bustling stock market. Similarly, both Spain and the United Kingdom have had multiple decades of struggle with home-grown terror organizations in the Basque ETA and the Northern Irish IRA, yet their economies have grown and prospered, the sovereign debt crisis notwithstanding. The United States too had its homegrown terrorists in the form of Ku Klux Clan in the South and the various leftist terror groups of the 1960s and early 1970s like the Symbionese Liberation Army of Patty Hearst fame, yet this period saw an enormous boom in the stock market. And of course, no listing of American terrorism would be complete without mentioning the Timothy McVeigh attack in 1995—which, as terrifying as it was, did virtually nothing to slow down the economic boom that the country was enjoying at the time.

Though it is horrifying to see the aftermath of an attack, investors tend to have short memories, and the economy and financial markets have a way of recovering. Life does go on. Terrorism—abhorrent though it is—just doesn't matter that much past the short term.

But what about war? War is a little more complicated, of course. Its effects on the stock and bond markets depend on the country's chances of winning. The United States enjoyed a massive bull market throughout World War II and the years that followed. But Japan? Well, not so much.

A prolonged and exceptionally expensive war can sap investor enthusiasm. But again, not always. American stocks did not fare particularly well during the Vietnam War era, but this was due more to the rampant inflation and other economic dislocations of the era, not the war, per se. Returning to the 1990s again, former President Bill Clinton had a very militarily-active presidency, though none of his campaigns had much of an effect on the stock market.

In none of the examples mentioned above was the freedom or security of the United States at significant risk. None of these were wars for survival, not even World War II. The United States could afford to have a war or two go the wrong way because, for the most part, the wars were taking place far from our shores. Of course, if a war or disruptive attack were severe enough, your stock portfolio would be the last thing on your mind.

The Rise of China: What Does it Mean?

According to Steven Rosefielde and D. Quinn Mills, authors of Masters of Illusion: American Leadership in the Media Age:

> *Woodrow Wilson made a basic mistake at the end of World War I and thereby contributed to the making of World War II. He believed that the dissatisfaction of minorities within polygot empires was the basic cause of the war (after all, didn't a Serbian nationalist assassinate the heir to the throne of the Austrian Empire and thereby occasion the war?) So he worked for the dissolution of the Austrian and European parts of the Russian empire, but left the German empire (made up of a single nationality) intact. Thus, he surrounded Germany with weak states, providing the temptation and opportunity for Hitler. We are in danger of doing the same now. We are taking our eyes off the great powers, and looking instead at issues like terrorism.*

The greatest power in question is, of course, China. With the fall of the Berlin War and the discrediting of communist ideology, there was a popular belief that we had reached "The End of History," in Francis Fukuyama's words. With no more ideological divisions, capitalist liberal democracy would be the ruling order of the day. There would be rogue states, of course. But the days of great power rivalry were over. After all, the world's economies are intertwined. Coca-Cola is sold throughout the world, McDonald's is in 119 countries across six continents and we buy more foreign-made cars than our own. We're basically all on the same team now; why would we need to fight?

Long before the "isms" of the 19th and 20th centuries (communism, fascism, Nazism, etc.) there were rivalries between the monarchies and republican movements in Europe. Before that, there were wars of religion between Protestants and Catholics and between Christians and Muslims. But before any of this, there were simple conflicts between states, kings, warlords or even between tribes for money, power and influence. This is the oldest form of great power rivalry, and it has always been a contributing factor to the ideological ones.

The problem with the Fukuyama argument is that pre-World War I Europe largely enjoyed similar conditions. The Continent was at peace and had largely been so since the close of the Napoleonic Wars in 1815. The royal families of Europe knew each other and most were related to one another ("inbred" might be a more accurate description, truth be told). Republican France had no axe to grind with its monarchical neighbors. This was the first golden age of globalization and free trade, and Europe was becoming wealthy—and it ended in an orgy of bloodshed in the worst war the world had ever seen.

So, is war with China inevitable? Absolutely not. But tensions are rising. With the United States distracted in the Middle East and with its domestic economic problems, China has become more assertive in other parts of the world. China is also quickly expanding its army and is building a blue-water navy. China's economy has also recently surpassed Japan's to become the second largest in the world. Whether or not we have war, we certainly have to deal with a more powerful and more assertive China.

Are America's Days of Global Dominance Numbered?

It has become popular to speak of the decline of the West and of the United States in particular. Titles like Fareed Zakaria's The

Post-American World have become commonplace. (While Zakaria's book was less about America's decline and more about "the rise of the rest," its gloomy title certainly fits the growing consensus.) Regardless of whether America is waxing or waning, we will undoubtedly have to make room at the table for some new, emerging powers. The two most commonly cited "emerging powers," China and India, have populations that are both massive and rapidly expanding. Does this make them a shoe-in at the top of the heap? Though their size may be advantageous—demographics will be important to these coming shifts—innovation and technology will be the driving forces. After all, some of the greatest world powers in history were small, technologically-savvy nations or even small city-states. Looking back, it may be hard to believe that the British Empire, which straddled the globe, was administered by a small, rainy island in the North Atlantic. Rome, the greatest empire of classical times, started out as an ambitious city. And well into the late Middle Ages, tiny Venice was the most powerful maritime country in Europe—and was the primary power holding the mighty Turkish Ottoman Empire at bay.

Neil Howe, who previously co-wrote several groundbreaking books on demographic trends with William Strauss (Generations, The Fourth Turning, Millennials Rising), published a new book in 2008 with Richard Jackson: The Graying of the Great Powers: Demography and Geopolitics in the 21st Century. What do Jackson and Howe have to say on the matter?

> The population and GDP of the United States, due to its relatively high fertility and immigration rates, will expand steadily as a share of the developed-world totals. In tandem, the influence of the United States within the developed world will likely rise. Many of today's multilateral theorists look forward to a global order in which the U.S. influence diminishes. In fact, any reasonable demographic projection points to a growing U.S. dominance among the developed nations that preside over this global order.

I would agree with Zakaria to an extent that the U.S. will need to allow up-and-comers like China, India and Brazil in to the "inner circle". But as Zakaria, Jackson, and Howe would all seem to agree, the United States will remain the preeminent economic, diplomatic and military force in the world for the foreseeable future.

Are Europe's Demographic Trends Reversible?

All demographers would agree that the West's and particularly Europe's low birthrates point to serious economic difficulties in the future. The question then becomes, are these demographic trends reversible? Or is Europe truly entering a demographic death spiral from which it will never recover? Some European countries have witnessed modest increases in their birthrates in recent years, even if the overall rate remains dangerously low. Jackson and Howe explain, "Notwithstanding the higher fertility rate of immigrants, most demographers do not believe that the recent uptick in fertility heralds a major turnaround in the long-term trend. In most countries, it appears to be the result of a temporary 'timing shift' that will soon run its course."

So as countries go through a period of modernization, the birthrate gets temporarily depressed due to women extending their educations and careers and postponing motherhood. A given woman may indeed still have the "normal" two to three kids over her lifetime; it's just that she gets started at 30 instead of 22.

Once this timing shift is complete, the fertility rate will recover to some extent. This is precisely what happened in the United States. Using Jackson and Howe's statistics, "after plunging from 3.7 in the mid-1950s to 1.7 in the mid 1970s, the U.S. fertility rate rose to 2.0 by the early 1990s under the impact of late-birthing Baby Boomers, where it has remained ever since."

In some of the European countries with the lowest fertility rates, such as Spain, Italy and Greece, it is likely that the timing shift is not yet complete. These traditionally "macho" countries started the process much later. So, each of these countries may enjoy a mini baby boom as this first generation of post-traditional women finally have children. But, as Jackson and Howe continue, "the potential to raise fertility is limited. In the United States, baby boomers only recuperated a fraction of the births in their 30s and 40s that they did not have in their 20s—and European women are unlikely to fare much better."

Spain, Italy and Greece may return to something close to the replacement rate of 2.1 children per woman from their current apocalyptically low rates of around 1.3. But the days of the large Mediterranean family are most likely over.

Can Pro-Natal Policies—Such as Child Tax Credits—Make a Difference?

The evidence is pretty convincing that pro-natal policies are largely ineffective in the modern, consumer-oriented economy. When the cultural and economic climate changes from one that favors a large family to one that favors a small family, there is not much the government can do about it. Will a child tax credit of a couple thousand dollars compensate a parent for the tens or hundreds of thousands of dollars in direct expenses? What about the untold thousands of dollars in lost wages and career opportunities (particularly for women who get "mommy tracked")? And what about lifestyle issues, such as the ability to take an unplanned trip to the Caribbean? The obvious answer is no; people who decide to have children believe that doing so has non-monetary benefits, and government incentives are not a major factor in their decision. This is what Jackson and Howe have to say on the matter:

> *Until recently, ideal fertility—that is the number of children that women say is optimal—remained at or above replacement in every developed country, even as actual fertility rates fell far beneath it. This suggested that there might be room for a substantial rebound if more supportive policies simply allowed women to actualize their ideal. But in a growing number of countries, including Austria, Italy, and Germany, ideal fertility has now dropped well beneath replacement. What has happened, according to some demographers, is that young adults in today's lowest-fertility countries, having spent their entire lives in societies where children are rare, have acquired a "culture of low fertility."*

Despite this, Jackson and Howe strongly recommend aggressive pro-natal policies such as those used in France and the Scandinavian countries. It is fair to ask: given the seriousness of the problem, doesn't it make sense to give it a try?

What Effects Will Aging Demographics Have on the Culture and Economy?

As you might expect, younger societies are full of dynamism, which is manifested by risk taking and an optimistic outlook. An older society, in contrast, becomes more conservative and risk averse. Productivity, progress and mobility slow. This has been Japan's experience and it fits neatly into Jackson and Howe's theory. They continue:

> When economists and historians try to describe the special economic vitality that often characterizes eras of high versus low population growth—the nineteenth century versus the fifteenth century in Europe, for example, for example, or 1960s versus the 1930s—they often allude to a contrast in a mood that cannot be reduced to a strictly classical analysis of the production function. The classical analysis, indeed, usually argues that a stationary or declining population should translate into economic performance (by lifting the ration of labor to land and to other fixed natural resources). Yet eras of high population growth have their own special attributes that are harder to define within standard theory—a restlessness mobility, urgency and optimism.

Note: I argued against this classical view earlier in this book in my discussion of Gregory Clark's A Farewell to Alms and David Hackett Fischer's The Great Wave. Continuing with Jackson and Howe,

> John Maynard Keynes and his U.S. counterpart Alvin H. Hansen always emphasized the role of population growth in triggering what Keynes called the "animal spirits" of investors. John Hicks, in his famous review of Keynes' General Theory, remarked: "Expectation of a continually expanding market, made possible by increasing population, is a fine thing for keeping up the spirits of entrepreneurs. With increasing population investment can

go roaring ahead, even if invention is rather stupid; increasing
population is therefore actually favorable to employment...
Perhaps the whole Industrial Revolution of the last two hundred
years has been nothing else but a vast secular boom, largely
induced by the unparalleled rise in population."

The modern economy depends on population growth. For an economy to grow, it needs more spenders. That's what we had in the 1980s and 1990s with the baby boomers. However, when a nation transforms from net spender to net saver, as the U.S. has been doing since the early 2000s, its economy contracts. To give a simplistic example, how can Ford sell more cars when there are fewer people of driving age to sell to? The only modern economy that has ever dealt with an aging and shrinking population is, of course, Japan. And as Japan's recent experience has shown, there is no real solution to this problem. There is no substitute for people.

Parting Thoughts

Richard Jackson and Neil Howe are not revolutionary in their writing of The Graying of the Great Powers; they are certainly not reinventing the wheel of demographic analysis. That said, Graying is an excellent collection of statistics and solid analysis of the major demographic issues that will shape the decades to come. For readers looking for a "big picture" book that will help them in their understanding of the world—and possibly their investments as well— Jackson and Howe's latest deserves a place on the bookshelf.

As investors, it is good to understand geopolitical trends, of course. Even though demographics tend to be more important from a macro perspective, whoever comes up with the next great technological innovation or has the most innovators will lead the world in the future. That is precisely why you see a big push for "green" industries and clean technology. That's one of the possible industries that will employ millions of people, thus providing an economic boom for their country. In the short term however, it ultimately all comes down to the price you pay: At a given price, are you being properly compensated for the risk you are taking? In the next chapter, I'll go into some of the details of my wealth management practice. At the risk of giving away some of my trade secrets, I'll explain my processes and offer insight on how to best approach your own investments.

CHAPTER 13:

HOW TO MAKE MONEY IN ANY MARKET

There is little doubt that we are in an economic pickle for the next several years, which will foster an extended period of low inflation and possibly outright deflation. In fact, without the magnitude of government intervention through economic stimulus, deflation would already be prevalent. This is very much contrary to the pervading view these days, but the research speaks for itself.

Even today, Janet Yellen and her financial puppeteers (the guys who are printing the money) are telling us to take our money out of savings and invest it, or be guaranteed a loss (after inflation and taxes). They are keeping rates low to force you to invest your money.

Only a flexible, active allocation has been demonstrated to add true value over market cycles. A static allocation or a "buy-and-hold" approach simply rides higher on the incoming tide and falls along with the outgoing tide. You are effectively trusting your financial future to the whims of an uncertain market. It's a lot like playing a game of craps. Your fortune will go up and it will go down, and the timing on when you need to walk away from the table will decide how much money you have left. The proof is in the pudding, as this approach got crushed during the recent crisis and has little to show for the past 10-12 years, now called the "lost decade."

In sharp contrast, a "hands-on tactical" or active allocation approach, much like our *Top-Down Tactical* (TDT™) strategy, seeks to outperform during rising markets by being invested in the leading asset classes and avoiding the laggards that drain performance, and then preserve those gains during the inevitable market declines by having a defensive risk management and exit strategy. In reserve, we have AssetLock™.

In this kind of economic environment, investors must employ an active tactical approach to investing. Old fashioned buy-and-hold, which I like to call buy-and-hope, is dead. Only during prolonged periods of bull markets can this approach work and that is clearly not our environment today or any time soon. That strategy really is your grandfather's Oldsmobile.

In a tactical approach, you may have a baseline portfolio allocation, but you're certainly not married to it. Instead, you have the ability to shift your money between asset classes or out of the markets altogether as conditions warrant. Going to cash can save you a lot of headaches and heart attacks. Even in the worst of long-term bear markets, there are stretches where certain sectors or the market as a whole do quite well. Using a tactical approach, you can participate in market rallies while sitting out some of the bear market corrections.

Let me give you a practical example. During the most intense moments of the 2008 crisis, I spent day and night (I couldn't sleep anyway) focusing on how to take advantage of the situation. What transpired was perhaps the greatest set of trades I have made in my career. I began buying the bonds and preferred stocks of companies the day it was announced that they were recipients of TARP funds.

Don't get me wrong, I was scared to death. Most investors and advisors alike were afraid to do anything, but I knew my clients were counting on me. as my good friend Tom always says, "Don't let a good crisis go to waste." I knew there were risks involved in the trades, but the risks were calculated. After all, risk must be managed properly, not avoided, otherwise you will not only always guarantee yourself a loss to purchasing power, but you will never get to take advantage of good opportunities as they come along. My thought was that once the government became a company's partner, so to speak, they would not be allowed to fail. Sure, the stockholders may languish, but that was not my concern. I owned the bonds and preferred stock, not the regular common stock, and as long as the company simply survived, my clients would collect their interest payments and get their principal return.

So, with the help my gifted bond trader Mike, I embarked on buying these TARP recipient company bonds and preferreds for clients. I took large positions in Goldman Sachs, American Express, HSBC, Bank of America and GMAC. I didn't have to buy securities with long maturities— usually just 2-4 years—and I was locking in yields of 15%–20%. With the preferreds I received the same yield as well as a big kicker as the prices of these doubled or tripled. Wow, what a coup. I still get goose bumps today when I think about it.

Although situations like these are few and far between, it's important to keep a sharp eye out for these types of opportunities, or work with someone who does and knows what to look for. In this current environment, you do not want investments that depend solely on rising prices. This includes most "growth stocks" as well as real estate and commodities.

As for what does work in a period of extremely low inflation or deflation, I have a one-word answer: income. After all, if you are not collecting some form of income from your investments, you are at the whim of the market. When prices are stagnant or falling, the income received from a stable investment like bonds, dividend-paying stocks, MLPs, REITs or annuities become all the more attractive. Pay yourself first.

The process that I go through when building an individual financial plan is very structured and disciplined. I take a holistic approach to wealth management for each individual client, never taking a one-size-fits-all or swing-for-the-fences approach. Wealth management is a comprehensive life plan, incorporating all the phases of your life and your family's life, whether you intend to spend every last nickel, give what's left to the kids, or donate it to charity.

It all starts with a written master plan is a must that incorporates all the major goals for a successful retirement and make sure you can cover future inflation, the rising cost of health care and increasing taxes, such as creating a retirement income stream that you and your spouse cannot outlive, understanding little-known tax strategies in retirement, how to optimize Social Security so you get every nickel you are entitled to, implementing a marginal tax distribution strategy to make sure when you initiate your sequence of distribution you stay in the lowest tax bracket possible forever.

Of course, the cornerstone of every master retirement plan is your portfolio. So when building a portfolio that will fund your plan, it is essential to take the least amount risk possible.

Step One: Determine the Required Rate of Return

As Yogi Berra once quipped, "If you don't know where you are going, you will wind up somewhere else." If you don't know what rate of return you are targeting, how will you know if your portfolio is appropriate and if your overall strategy is working? Frequently, investors incorrectly compare their success to an index like the Dow Jones Industrial Average or the S&P 500. Most people do not want or need all the risk that the stock market possesses, nor should they take it. Oftentimes, investors simply need to keep pace with purchasing power (inflation and taxes), yet they subject themselves to sleepless nights and broken dreams by taking on more risk than they think they need. Determining your required rate of return is the most crucial step.

In order to reach this number, we work backward—starting with your end goal in mind. We know how much money you have today; that part is easy. After putting a pencil to it, we calculate how much you need to have at crucial points in your life. After figuring the number of years you have to reach that point, the rate of return you need to meet your needs becomes an easy "plug-in" number.

As you get closer to retirement, downside protection with an exit strategy becomes critical. It becomes effectively impossible to make the money back if you lose it to a major bear market, a correction or a supposedly rare black swan event. Invest for need, not for greed™.

Step Two: Determine the Risk Tolerance

After determining your required rate of return, the focus turns to the subject of risk. Specifically, how much risk we must assume in order to reach our required return. The answer is simply to take the very least amount of risk necessary to achieve your objectives. Period. Greed always takes over when we think about how much we "could" make if everything went perfectly. It's often not until the market crashes do we realize that we are taking too much risk.

Step Three: Determine the Broad Allocation

The goal of allocation optimization is to find the portfolio, which offers the highest expected return for a given amount of risk or the least amount of risk for a given level of return. I spent my early years with brokerage firms that heavily influenced and kept strict control over what we invested in and taught us to invest in stocks, bonds and cash—and to stay invested. That was it! There wasn't much discussion about alternative investments. I also recall that an aggressive portfolio had something like 85% in stocks and a moderate to aggressive portfolio had 70% in stocks. There was no personal attention whatsoever. In fact, you see many people today get swayed by these so called "personal portfolio management" programs which are nothing more than glorified mutual funds. In a true customized investment plan, your portfolio must be tailor-made for your personal situation with regards to everything from risk to taxes, and each holding must be just right for you individually.

Of course, no one really complains when their portfolio makes too much money. But if you were holding that much in stocks when the recent bear came knocking, your portfolio got mauled. Moreover, if you lost 50% in a year, you would need to earn 100% just to break even. Therefore, in my view, managing the downside risk is the single most important thing I can do for my client's portfolio. Any plan must have a personal exit strategy. Unfortunately, many investors learned this the hard way in the recent crisis.

Therefore, in portfolio construction, I search for assets with a good risk/return relationship and a low correlation to each other, as well as assets with a low correlation to the broader stock market. My ultimate goal is to find the combination of assets that protects well on the downside and lets the upside take care of itself.

Keep in mind, if you have sufficient assets to build your own fund, you should do so. For many investors, and certainly for wealthy investors, you should avoid owning traditional mutual funds, except for special situations such as for specific short-term sector allocations. Mutual funds have tremendous disadvantages. They are illiquid because they are only priced once a day. There are "gotcha" phantom taxes on gains, an added layer of fees and no personal management to represent your financial interests.

In short, I build my client's own personal no-load fund. There are no fees in or out, no commissions on stock or bond transactions, and if we use a mutual fund there are never any loads. If the fund has a load, the load is waived. This puts me on the same team as my client.

Step Four: Select the Subcategories

After we determine the broad allocation, we must choose the subcategories. Most of us are taught early to diversify over a number of categories. What I've learned is that simple diversification alone does not necessarily protect in a major panic like 2008. You have to stay nimble and tactical, and part of that is choosing the right mix of subcategories.

Stocks. I favor different categories or sectors depending on economic and market conditions. Once it's decided as to how much will be allocated to stocks, the next allocation is made toward how much goes into each sector: large, mid, small cap, value, growth or blend. I often use Exchange Traded Funds (ETFs) as they provide the ability to select a specific sector and sub-sector that do not correlate with the other sectors. Too often people believe they are diversified just by owning a lot of stocks or mutual funds only to find out that they correlate too much or the funds all own the same underlying stocks. Your investments must adapt to changing market conditions. I also will get out of all stocks and into cash during dangerous periods.

Bonds. For bonds, I invest in the best after-tax returns with the shortest maturities available. My goal here is to achieve a positive return with the bonds no matter how interest rates are trending. Currently I'm getting close to double-digit yields in short-term bonds with maturities of just five years, so why take the risk that comes with longer-dated bonds? I go into deeper detail on bonds in Chapter 13.

Alternative Investments. Although real estate in the form of real estate investments trusts (REITs) could easily be included in the stock category, I use it here. Others include managed futures, Master Limited Partnerships with dividends that are 85% tax-free, currency ETFs, options (especially covered calls), commodity funds and ETFs, and long-short or market neutral funds. I am seeking assets that are not highly correlated with the broader stock market.

Step Five: Select the Specific Holdings

In selecting the specific holdings, I have many tools at my disposal that are not available to individuals or are cost prohibitive for many of them, such as: the institutional version of Morningstar Office; Lowry's Independent Research, which has been around since 1938 and provides the best technical analysis I know of; Bloomberg; Allocation Master; Zacks; and JPMorgan research to name just a few. My 25+ years in the business allows me to find things that others can't. The specifics will depend directly on the current economic and market environment, and my outlook for the short, intermediate and long term.

Step Six: Implement the Portfolio

Tactical asset allocation is hands-on portfolio management that over-weights and under-weights different market allocations based on market conditions, as well as utilizing cash during dangerous times. A buy-and-hold asset allocation style dictates buying many investment categories and holding them regardless of market conditions. I think that's ludicrous. Our trademarked Top-Down Tactical (TDT™) investment management strategy is built for today's economic environment.

Step Seven: Monitor the Portfolio

When monitoring the portfolio, I constantly examine the broad allocation as well as the underlying holdings. Although I conduct comprehensive client reviews quarterly, I am constantly monitoring each account. The bottom line to me is the advisor's version of the Hippocratic Oath, "Provide safety, security and peace of mind."

The Joy of Dividends

Here, I want to get a little philosophical talking about dividends. Dividends are essential for every serious investor. Speculators don't need them, gamblers wouldn't touch them, but genuine long-term investors can't live without them. Dividends have accounted for almost 50% of the S&P 500's returns since 1925 and over 100% for the last decade.

Though the focus of this section is stock dividends, the analysis is applicable for all income-oriented investments, be they common stocks, preferred stocks, REITs, bonds or just about any investment that enhances its return by distributing capital back to its investors. These investments do well when the market does well but, more importantly, they outperform when the stock market is either flat or down, providing steady income and downside protection. Capital gains can be ephemeral; income is real.

Investors who ignore dividends are essentially gambling. As I previously mentioned, building a portfolio of investments that does not provide any income is not too different from playing craps. You will go up, you will go down, and the timing of when you walk away from the table (i.e., needing the money to retire) will decide how much money you have. Pity the poor retirees of the last decade, because if they needed their money to live on over the last 10–12 years, it is likely that their retirement dreams—along with their portfolios—have vanished.

Preferred stock is an asset class many investors do not understand. Preferred stock may be a great investment option for income, but the word "stock" in the name is often misleading. Although these "stocks" can trade on the major stock exchanges, they are really fixed-income investments that have more in common with bonds or CDs than with common stocks. The dividend payments for preferred stocks are set when the shares are issued and generally do not vary. Most of them become callable five years after they are issued. This means that if interest rates fall, a company can take back the shares and pay you the price at which they were issued.

Many analysts agree that one of the positives of preferreds has been their relatively stable share price, although they do fluctuate. That stability comes from knowing the level of future dividends, as long as the companies continue to meet all of their debt obligations. With common stock, by contrast, companies can cut dividends during lean times without any warning. Generally, preferreds are susceptible to the same risk factors as bonds, like inflation and rising interest rates. For the most part, if a company misses earnings estimates, that might affect the common stock,

but not the preferreds. However, if a company is at legitimate risk of financial distress or bankruptcy, even preferred dividends can be cut. This happened to several companies in 2008, and investors who believed their investments were conservative got a rude awakening.

For the individual investor, preferreds are generally easier to own than individual bonds. Preferreds can be bought and sold on the major exchanges through virtually any broker, rather than in the bond market, which is less liquid and transparent. And shares are usually priced at $25 each when they are issued, versus the $1,000 price for most new corporate bonds.

For tax purposes, there are two flavors of preferred stocks. Many preferreds have dividends that are eligible for the qualified dividend tax rate—15% for most investors—because the dividends are paid with after-tax dollars, while others pay dividends that are taxed at an investor's federal income tax rate. The companies write off these payments, so from the perspective of the IRS, they are more like the interest that is paid to corporate bondholders.

Sometimes preferreds do not pay qualified dividends but yield a bit more than those that do, so these may be better to hold in tax-advantaged accounts like IRAs. However, if the dividend is high enough even after you pay the taxes, as is often the case, a non-

Figure 13.1 Return Generator by Time Horizon (S&P 500)

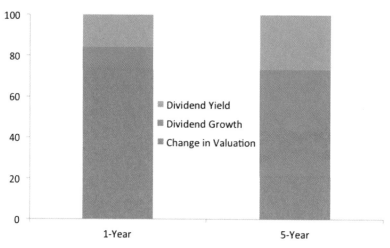

Source: James Montier, "A Man From a Different Time"

Figure 13.2: Return Generator by Time Horizon (S&P 500)

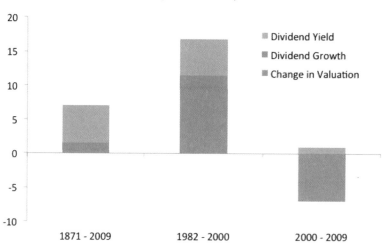

Source: James Montier, "A Man From a Different Time"

retirement account is just fine. After all, it's not what you make but what you keep that counts. If you are buying an individual security, the prospectus will say whether it pays qualified dividends.

Preferred stocks can be a great addition to your portfolio, whether you are looking to get a higher yield than CDs or money markets, or to provide stability to your portfolio in a volatile market.

A Man from a Different Time

James Montier of GMO has done excellent work on common stock dividends. I recommend you browse his recent white paper "A Man from a Different Time," available for free on the GMO website (www. gmo.com). In this section, I am going to share with you some of the insights from
that paper.

In doing an exhaustive study of stock returns going back to 1871, Montier reached several conclusions. Some are obvious, but others will likely come as a surprise to you. In a given year, nearly 80% of the real total return is generated by changes in stock valuation, with the remainder coming from the dividend yield and the growth rate of dividends (see **Figure 13.1**). This makes sense, of course. Stock prices regularly have intra-year swings of 30% or more. As your time horizon expands, however, fundamentals like dividends become far more important. Montier found that at even a short five-year time horizon, it is dividend yield and dividend growth that account for almost 80% of the return, with changes in valuation accounting for barely 20%.

Over longer periods, dividends account for a full 90% of real total returns (see the first bar on **Figure 13.2**). Interestingly, something changed during the 1982–2000 period. During this "cult of equity" period in which the Baby Boomers accumulated their investment nest eggs, dividends were deemphasized in favor of share buybacks, acquisitions or the accumulation of cash on corporate balance sheets. Capital gains became the primary driver of investor returns, which made sense for tax reasons but also led to the rise of a gambling mentality that has since wreaked havoc on the market.

Of course, for everything there is a season. Dividends were the only source of return during the 2000–2009 period. Stock price returns were negative for the period.

What are we to take away from all of this? Though tax policy will have an effect on returns going forward, dividends should be a major focus of your investment strategy whether you are a young investor just beginning to accumulate assets or an experienced investor in or nearing retirement. That is simply where the sweet spot is in the current market, providing the best returns with the least risk possible.

If you don't need the income now for current needs, reinvest your dividends to accelerate the compounding process. By doing this, you raise the odds that you can generate respectable returns even in a bear market. Dividend reinvestment is a form of dollar-cost averaging, and corrections and bear markets actually work to your advantage over time. If the value of your shares suffers a short-term setback, your dividend payments allow you to buy more shares at a cheaper price.

As always, use common sense. Investors who chased high dividends in the form of banks, finance companies and business development companies saw much of their investment wiped out in 2008. Never buy a stock simply because the dividend yield is high, but always consider the dividend as a major source of long-term returns.

The Nuts and Bolts of Dividend Investing

There are a lot of misconceptions about dividends, and I aim to clear them up. Dividend investing is not just about generating income for living expenses. Frankly, if that is all you need, you can create "synthetic" dividends by selling off a given dollar amount of stock every month and living off the proceeds.

No, dividend investing is much more. It's a managerial mindset and an important signal to investors. A management team that makes paying a dividend a priority is a management team that has its shareholders in mind. It shows that management knows its place. They are there to make you money, not to build empires for themselves or get on the front page of the Wall Street Journal. It's a subtle but important distinction.

Paying a cash dividend also forces discipline on management. Nothing is more devastating to a stock than having to cut its dividend. Knowing they have a quarterly payout to make, managers are less likely to take undue risk.

With that, let's dig into some common questions.

What is the ex-dividend date? And if I wanted to earn a quick buck, couldn't I buy a stock immediately before it goes ex-dividend and then sell it immediately after?

The ex-dividend date is the date of record for collecting the dividend. In other words, whoever owns a share of stock on the ex-dividend date is entitled to receive the dividend. They can sell it the very next day and still expect to receive the dividend payment on the payment date, which could be days or weeks later.

But buying a stock immediately before its ex-div date and selling immediately after is not a viable way to generate income. A dividend represents a disbursement of value, and a stock will generally fall in value on its ex-dividend date by an amount roughly equal to the dividend. For example, if a stock declares a $1 dividend, the share price will fall by about a dollar on its ex-dividend date to reflect that loss of the value being distributed.

It's a fundamental law of economics: There is no free lunch.

In any event, I wouldn't encourage short-termism when investing for income. There is nothing wrong with short-term trading, but you should always maintain an income-paying core of investments that you can live on if your trading hits a rough patch.

Master Limited Partnerships (MLPs) often pay massive distributions that are tax-free. Is this too good to be true?

199

Again, there is no free lunch. MLPs do not pay "tax-free dividends." But MLPs—and particularly those in oil and gas—often pay distributions that are untaxable in the year they are paid. This is not semantics; it's actually an important tax point.

Remember, dividends are a distribution of profit. If a company pays out more in dividends that it makes in earnings, they are essentially just returning your original investment to you. This is what is called a "return of capital," and it is very common with MLPs. All or most of a given MLP distribution can be considered return of capital. REIT dividends also often have a smaller portion that is considered return of capital, though this is uncommon with regular dividend-paying stocks.

When you receive a return of capital distribution, you're not avoiding taxes forever. The distribution simply lowers your cost basis, meaning that when you eventually sell you will have to realize more in taxable capital gains.

The one exception? If you die. At this point, you really do get a "free lunch" of sorts, in that your heirs see the cost basis reset and thus have no unrealized capital gains to worry about. Of course, this doesn't change the fact that
you're dead!

I'm worried about the new "ObamaCare surtax" on investment income. Will that affect my dividend-paying investments?

Yes, or at least it can if you or your spouse has a high income. The new 3.8% surtax, which went into effect last year and was included in the Patient Protection and Affordable Care Act, applies to single taxpayers with modified adjusted gross incomes of $200,000 or more. The threshold jumps to $250,000 for couples that are married and filing jointly. The 3.8% tax is applied to the lesser of your total "investment-related income," which includes dividends, or your modified adjusted gross income over the threshold amounts listed above.

Also, remember that the regular tax on dividends rose from 15% to

20% for single taxpayers with incomes above $400,000 and married couples with incomes over $450,000. So, a high-income taxpayer could pay as much as 23.8% on qualified dividends.

For this reason, I recommend holding dividend-paying stocks in an IRA or other tax-advantaged account if you have the ability to do so. You should prioritize, however. Bond interest and capital gains on collectibles are taxed at even higher rates, so these assets should be the first ones you put in an IRA, followed by REITs and dividend-paying stocks. Assets that pay little income and that are held for long-term capital gains should be the last assets you put in an IRA, as they are the most tax efficient.

CHAPTER 14:

WHAT TO RUN AND HIDE FROM

I am generally an optimist, and I like to focus on the positive. Frankly, I find this to be a far healthier and more profitable way to live my life. Nearly all successful people are at heart optimists, almost to a fault. If you think about it, you would have to be an optimist to start a business or to be successful in your career. You've probably worked with chronic pessimists before. Frankly, they're buzzkills, and it's easy to let them drag you down. Those with negative or fatalistic attitudes tend to not go very far in life… which only seems to make their negativity worse.

So, it is natural that I tend to focus on what investments I think will do well in the years ahead instead of focusing on what investments I think will do poorly. But I think it is also important to mention assets I think you should specifically avoid. After all, the best way to win in investing is to avoid losing. One bad bear market can reverse years or even decades of steady gains. We all know that investors with large positions in tech stocks in 2000 or financial stocks in 2008 would have been a lot better off had they avoided those unfortunate sectors.

I'll start with bonds. I consider the bond market to be extremely risky right now, arguably riskier than the stock market. As I've driven home in this book, I expect market yields to stay lower than usual for years to come. But they could rise quite a bit from today's levels and still be very low by historical averages.

Rising bond yields mean falling bond prices, and this is more true the longer the bond's maturity. If you own individual bonds, this is not necessarily a problem. If you're confident in the ability of the borrower to pay, you can simply hold the bond to maturity. You may lose a little purchasing power to inflation, but you have no risk of capital loss.

This is not true of bond mutual funds, however. A bond mutual fund is presumed to have a perpetual life, meaning that you will almost certainly lose money if yields rise from here. Current bond yields are not high enough to compensate you for a drop in prices.

Now, there is one exception here. Tactical bond fund managers will actively buy and sell bonds. Managers like Bill Gross and Jeff Gundlach have been doing it for decades and have built fantastic track records. But when you buy a tactical bond fund, you're not really investing in "bonds," per say. You're investing in the manager. So, if you go this route, make sure you're comfortable with the manager.

As I mentioned in the previous chapter, I'm generally a believer in keeping bond maturities shorter. With shorter-dated bonds, I avoid most of the interest rate risk.

Bottom line: As a general rule, stay away from long-only bond mutual funds. To the extent you own bonds, either buy individual bonds or go with a solid tactical manager. And go with shorter-maturity bonds whenever possible.

Now I'd like to focus on the darling asset class of the last decade: commodities.

As I'm writing this chapter at the tail end of 2015, the price of crude oil has dropped by nearly half in less than six months. That's an outright crash, not just a run-of-the-mill bear market.

Weak demand from Europe and Japan was certainly a contributing factor in the selloff. But this was mostly a supply story. High global prices led to the great American energy renaissance, and the fracking revolution allowed the United States to rival Saudi Arabia and Russia as a major oil producer. Supply rising faster than demand, prices fall. That's how a market works.

Personally, I expect energy prices to find a bottom soon if they haven't already. I don't expect to see crude oil at $100 per barrel in the near future, as markets tend to rise a lot more slowly than they fall. But I do expect it to at least stabilize.

Commodities in general have had a great run over the past decade. With the global economy showing signs of recovery, there is renewed talk that demand from China and India will keep commodity prices high and rising for decades to come.

Really? Whenever I hear these kinds of arguments, I cringe a little. This is bad analysis. These same conditions were equally true 15 years ago, when prices were at multi-decade lows. As economies grow and mature, they do initially use more commodities, particularly energy. But they also become far more efficient in their use of commodities. Rising prices give them no other choice. Fuel efficiency is much higher today than in years past. With home heating and air conditioning prices as high as they are, homes are becoming more efficient, as are appliances.

The same is true of manufacturing processes. Consider the case of automobiles. Cars today use a lot less metal than they used to, having replaced it with cheaper, lighter materials. This is true of homes too, for that matter. Given how low incomes are in India and China, is it plausible that Indian and Chinese consumers and businesses will pay any price for the materials they need? I think not.

Let's now take a look at what is probably the single most important industrial metal: copper.

The picture looks bad for copper right now. Globally, new construction accounts for 44% of copper use. And given the size of China's construction industry, it's not too surprising that China accounts for 45% of total world demand. Consider Chinese copper ore imports over the past 10 years. They've grown by a factor of six, and we're talking about metric tons of the stuff, not the dollar price.

China is not an important part of the copper market. China is the copper market. Without a booming Chinese construction sector, there is no demand for copper, particularly with Japan in recession, most of Europe flirting with recession and the U.S. construction sector looking wobbly at best.

But here's the kicker. We actually don't need Chinese construction to completely grind to a halt in order to have a bear market in copper. Supply of new copper has outpaced demand for several years running, with much of the excess sitting in Chinese warehouses. Figures here are a little shadowy, but China's Strategic Reserves Bureau is believed to have purchased as much as 700,000 tons in the first nine months of 2014.

What is the Chinese government doing with it? Not a whole lot, it seems. They're keeping it in a strategic reserve to tap into in the event of a supply disruption, similar to the Strategic Petroleum Reserves here in the U.S.

The Chinese government isn't the only player in China with ample supplies. The fees that miners pay smelters to refine copper ore into refined metal have been rising, and Freeport McMoRan, the global miner, recently agreed to pay 16.3% more in processing costs to Chinese copper smelters. In other words, it's a buyer's market for copper smelters. Chinese smelters have more supply of ore than they need, so they can pretty well dictate prices to the miners.

I use copper as a high profile example, but the story is the same for many other commodities. As was the case with oil, the high prices of the late 2000s and early 2010s caused a surge of new production… which inevitably led to oversupply and falling prices. Yet most investors appear to be clueless about this and fail to understand that commodities aren't really an investment in the truest sense. As Peter Tasker put it in a Financial Times editorial,

> *Di-worse-ification is what you do when you invest in mediocre assets for a mediocre reason—for example, because a statistical model has told you they reduce risk. Thanks to the boom in commodities during the past decade, these have become a*

favored choice for di-worse-ifying institutions everywhere. The profusion of funds and exchange-traded funds, indices and brokerage coverage has made commodities unprecedentedly easy to access for individuals too. However, the long-term performance of commodities is pathetic, and there is little reason to believe that this time is different. [32]

Investors who piled into commodities at the end of the 1970s regretted it, and investors who are invest a large chunk of their assets in commodities today are unlikely to fare much better. In fact, there is a good case to be made that it is the investors themselves that contributed most to the run-up in prices. Many commodities are currently priced in "contango" and have been for years. Essentially, that means when too many investors try to buy the same futures contract at the same time, it forces up the price of that contract relative to longer-dated contracts on the same commodity. So, passive commodity investors who "roll over" their contracts on expiration get absolutely screwed. They buy the front-month contract high and sell it low... over and over again. If the spot price is in a strong uptrend and the contango is only mild, you might not notice. But if the market is flat or only mildly rising, you can actually lose a lot of money as the negative roll yield grinds away at the value of your account every month.

Most of the popular mutual funds and ETFs that track commodities suffer from this problem, and I'd be willing to bet a large sum of money that the investors buying these products have no idea this is the case.

Investors must also be conscious of the fact that quantitative easing by the Fed does create higher commodity prices through a lower dollar. It's like an artificial sweetener. Commodities are priced in dollars, so as the dollar goes down, commodity prices go up and imports cost more for the same reason. A lower dollar makes import prices rise. That made sense last decade. But today, the dollar is strong again, as investors have come to view the U.S. dollar as the cleanest dirty shirt among major world currencies.

Now, I should be clear on something. I'm recommending you stay away from commodities as a buy-and-hold investment, but I have nothing against shorter-term trading. And at the right price, commodities, including precious metals like gold, silver or platinum, can be effective as a currency or an apocalypse hedge. But as a general rule, it is best to view commodities as short-term trades and not long-term investments. I'll wrap up my commodity thoughts with another humorous quote from Mr. Tasker:

> *Commodities don't deserve to generate any return. As the name suggests, they are undifferentiated lumps of naturally occurring materials. Value needs to be added to them by the application of knowledge; it is investment in that process of application that earns the return. Over the long haul the price of the commodities themselves reverts to the cost of production.*
>
> *As societies become more sophisticated, knowledge generates ever greater returns. By contrast, societies in which commodities are highly valued are by definition primitive. That is why the price of copper peaked out in ancient Egyptian times, when a few kilograms could buy you a slave girl. Its purchasing power has been in decline ever since. In essence copper has been in a bear market for 3,000 years. Consider that before you di-worse-ify.*

I often get asked by clients what my opinion on real estate is. Is it an investment? Well, yes and no. It depends. But I can definitely say this: Your personal residence is not an investment.

There, I said it.

Buying a home might be a good financial decision, of course. It's certainly something you should consider in your overall financial plan. But I repeat: Your home is not an investment.

It's time to revisit housing. Home prices nationwide are continuing to recover after the bloodbath of the late 2000s.

But as home prices continue to recover, you need to keep a level head. I own my home, and it makes financial sense to do so. But I don't consider it an investment, and I live in a home that is modest relative to standard rules of thumb for income and net worth.

I'm going to share my guidelines for how to view housing as a part of a broader financial plan. But first, let's cover one very basic question: what is an investment? My strictest definition of an investment is something that pays an income today or that you expect will pay an income in the future, via dividends, interests, royalties, business profits, etc. (Raw land, art and collectibles are a grey area here; I consider these speculations rather than "investments.")

A home you purchase to use as a rental would certainly qualify as an investment. But your personal residence most certainly does not qualify. Rather than pay you an income, your personal residence is actually a source of regular expenses in the form of your mortgage payment, taxes, utilities and maintenance.

So, let me repeat one this critical point one last time: You shouldn't consider your home an investment.

That said, you should consider a home as part of your financial planning the same way you consider other budget items. Here are points to consider:

1. As an "investment," homes offer low rates of return. Yale economist Robert Shiller found that American home prices rose at about half a percent per year from 1890 to 2008 after adjusting for inflation. In contrast, most long-term studies have shown stocks to return about 7% per year after adjusting for inflation. And again, your primary residence is a source of regular expense, not income.

2. All else equal, buying is more sensible than renting in that it puts you on the right side of long-term inflation trends. Under normal conditions, apartment rent will rise every year due to regular inflation. But a 30-year mortgage payment will change only modestly due to rising taxes and insurance payments. The key here is "all else equal." Do not use this as an excuse to buy more house than you can afford.

Try to keep your house payment relatively close to what you would pay in rent.

3. Owning a home also builds equity over time, due to paying down your mortgage and due to natural price increases due to inflation. This is only true over very long time periods, however, measured in decades. Never buy a house with the intent of "flipping it" within a couple years unless you recognize that doing so is a high-risk speculation.

4. Don't be extravagant. If you are a family of two to four, you probably don't need a 3,500 square foot house. You're giving yourself a massive liability in terms of utilities and maintenance, not to mention a higher property tax bill and insurance payment. If you are wealthy, knock yourself out.

Buy the biggest, baddest house you can find, and enjoy it. It's your money, and you only live once. But if you are a regular American trying to build wealth over time, buy a modestly-sized house. You will save a ton of money over time and will have more income at your disposal to invest or
spend on yourself.

5. In terms of budget, the commonly quoted rule of thumb is that your mortgage payment should be about 30% of your gross (pre-tax) income. I think that is reasonable, but I would make that an absolute cap and I would recommend paying closer to 20% if that is realistic at your current income levels. Remember, every dollar that goes into your home is a dollar that cannot be spent or invested elsewhere.

6. Resist the temptation to constantly upgrade your house, even though, frankly, it's addictive. But it is also very expensive, and if you let it get out of control it can consume your entire budget. By all means, make modest improvements to the house, but consider this a hobby expense that comes out of your discretionary budget and not an "investment." Some projects—such as a kitchen or bathroom remodel—tend to be net positive creators of value in that they tend to raise the selling price higher than the cost of the project. But most

home projects break even at best, and many are actually net losses.

7. Unless you have a medical emergency, do not borrow against your home equity. Do not—I repeat, DO NOT—be seduced into extracting equity or taking on a home equity line of credit. These are far less common than they were pre-crisis, but I'm starting to see them advertised again. Borrowing against your home negates the equity you are building and is massively detrimental to your long-term wealth building.

Finally, there are non-monetary points to consider. Many people buy a home because they want to be a part of the community. Maybe they want a tree swing to push their kid on or a garage to tinker in.

I can't really put a dollar value on these things, and I wouldn't try. These are quality of life factors. But they do come at real dollar cost. Keep that in mind when doing your budgeting. Any marginal increase in expense from owning rather than renting should be accounted for as an "expense," not an investment. And if that means that you need to cut down on other lifestyle expenses, such as eating in restaurants, in order to meet your savings and investing goals, then so be it.

Now, a rental property is a very different kind of asset. A home purchased as a rental property does indeed qualify as an investment by my criteria, as it throws off income—and tax-advantaged income at that. But just because a property can be a good investment, that doesn't mean it's guaranteed. All markets are local, and all properties have their peculiar quirks. But as a general rule, I would ask the following questions when evaluating a property for investment purposes:

1. Is the property cash-flow positive from the beginning of the deal, or can you realistically expect to be cash-flow positive in the near future, perhaps pending modest renovations? If not, move on.

2. Capital appreciation is an important potential source of return, too. Are prices rising or falling in the neighborhood? If they are falling, why are they falling, and do you have reason to believe that

prices will soon recover? Ideally, a nice time to buy is after a price correction has ended and prices have started to creep up again.

3. What are the demographics of the neighborhood and of the surrounding area? What is the "demographic story?" For example, are young families moving to the neighborhood? Or is the neighborhood dominated by couples in late middle age with "empty nests?" You want to be on the right side of a demographic trend. This could mean buying in a retirement area that is attracting downsizing Baby Boomers. But my favorite demographic trend is the family formation of the Millennials. Starter homes and modest "trade-up" homes in cities attracting young workers are the best product area in which to invest. "McMansions" favored by high earners in middle age should be avoided, as these are the properties most likely to be offloaded by retiring Boomers. I see selling pressure in this product niche for the next decade.

The bottom line here is not to avoid real estate. It can be a fine asset class if done right. But be realistic and don't try to be the next Donald Trump.

Let's take one last look at the big picture. Investing is not just a matter of choosing the right (or wrong!) asset class. It's also about mindset. To wrap this chapter up with a laugh, I want to share Reformed Broker Josh Brown's list of the worst possible investor qualities... those that would create a Frankenstein's monster of an investor Obsesses over each day's activity.

1. Relentlessly judges self against benchmarks, picking and choosing which one "matters" on any given day.

2. Is preoccupied with other people's trades and quick to hurl insults at people who get things wrong.

3. Cannot tolerate the disagreement of other investors, takes personal offense and lashes out in the presence of dissent over an investment idea.

4. Attempts to assign meaning to every random fluctuation in the markets.

5. Constantly incorporating new data into a "master" thesis or theme, rejecting whatever doesn't fit.

6. Keeps a running score over who else was wrong or right over years and years.

7. Emphasizes winning trades in conversation as though they exist in isolation.

8. Plays for batting average (W's and L's) as opposed to the overall result, ignores trading costs, taxes and other tangible portfolio friction.

9. Frequently abandons an underperforming strategy when something else appears to be working better.

10. Blames larger forces for unsatisfactory results, i.e.: The Fed, Central Banking, Politicians, etc.

11. Adopts really strong opinions and defends them to the death.

12. Allows religious, political or social views to color (dominate?) their investment portfolio / strategy.

13. Uses tips from experts in lieu of research, misunderstands the difference between TV and real life.

14. Forgets that a stock or a fund doesn't know or care who its owners are, or what price they acquired it at; trades for revenge.

Well said, Mr. Brown. Let heed this advice and not slip into the same bad habits.

Conclusion

Whether you learn how to surf the economic tsunami or you get swept away with it is up to you. We're all a lot older and at least a little bit wiser. We have to be because we're not 20-something anymore. Life certainly changes. Even if you do have the time to make it back after the next crisis, why would you want to?

What a long strange trip it has certainly been. It seems like a lifetime since I searched for that coffee during those fateful days at the Arenal lodge in Costa Rica when the meteor—just seconds from impact—narrowly avoided earth. Since the market bottom in March 2009, stocks have soared, and the pain and hysteria that investors felt during that volatile period seems like a distant memory. Even some of the highest-profile casualties—such as General Motors—have been brought back from the dead. It's as if the crisis never happened. Life appears to be returning to normal… so far, that is. People's memories are much too short.

The government tells us that everything has been fixed and we are on the road to recovery, but I'm taking that with a healthy grain of salt. The meltdown and crisis of 2008 was caused by excessive debts in the financial and mortgage sectors. And while debt levels are slowly falling in these areas, government debt has exploded in response. I cannot imagine that years from now, when we look back on this period, the solution was to just print money and throw it into the economy without getting to the root of the problem: having too much debt to begin with. It looks an awful lot like trying to treat a recovering alcoholic with more of the hair of the dog that bit him!

There is no doubt that America is at a crossroads. The government may try to convince us that the crisis is over, but we're only half way through at best. Economic fundamentals, market cycles and demographic trends are all converging in such a way that threatens the long-term prosperity to which we Americans have become accustomed. The combination of Baby Boomers passing their peak spending years, an enormously over indebted consumer and a government in crisis over how to pay for entitlement programs is brewing up a storm of epic proportions, and it will affect the way you live and invest.

We've just gone through 20+ years of a borrowing and spending binge, and a massive wave of deleveraging is happening as a result. We had a great party; unfortunately, it left a killer hangover that we now have to suffer through.

The factors that make the spending spree of the 1990s and 2000s possible will not be repeated in the years ahead. Those Baby Boomers that fueled the boom in their early middle age are now past their peak spending years. Rather than act as gasoline on the economic fire, they will now act as a wet blanket. The next decade will see these Boomers saving every penny they can, and a penny saved is distinctly not a penny spent in the economy.

The second factor was easy lending. When the Boomers—and the rest of the country too, for that matter—ran out of money to spend, they simply borrowed more. With home prices rising and interest rates low, it was easy to extract equity from their homes. But with home prices still below their pre-crisis highs in many cities, there is very little equity left to extract. And even if there was, the battered banks are in very poor position to make loans. The same is true of credit card companies, auto finance companies, and anyone else who traditionally lends money to consumers.

And the government? With the budget deficit at record levels, the national debt spiraling out of control and the enormous Social Security and Medicare expenditures coming down the pipeline, how exactly is the government going to be in a position to help with any of this? You can be certain that it won't be. And even the Federal Reserve—that ultimate backstop—is essentially out of ammo. The Fed may not raise interest rates for longer than many think as growth continues to languish. We are now more than five years into the current economic expansion. I'm not forecasting an imminent recession, but in the entire span of U.S. history since the Great Depression the longest stretch we've ever gone without a recession was 10 years—and that was during the 1990s tech boom. Since the Great Depression, the average time between recessions was four years and nine months.

Again, I'm not necessarily predicting a major recession around the corner. But expansions do not last forever, and we should remember that our current expansion has been aided by record federal deficits and the loosest monetary policy in U.S. history. I think it's highly likely that we will indeed see a recession at some point in the next two years, and this time around the Fed will have fewer options at its disposal. When traditional monetary policy failed to do the trick in 2012, we got "QE Infinity," and open-ended plan to buy $85 billion per month in government and mortgage bonds. As politically unpopular as it was, I don't see it being repeated again.

The government response has given us a federal budget deficit that would rival a Banana Republic, mortgaging our children's future (sorry Josh), on the cheap. It's nothing more than a giant Ponzi scheme. The sad part is that it has had little net effect on the economy because private sector deleveraging is more than offsetting the government stimulus.

Yet the stock market continues to rise, largely because of a lack of anywhere else for investors to go. Savings accounts, CDs, and money market accounts yield next to nothing, and even longer-term bonds barely keep pace with inflation. Even the companies themselves are buying their own stock for lack of better options. With expansion plans on hold for most of the past six years, companies have been pouring their excess cash into share repurchases. That's not a bad thing, mind you. I'm actually a big fan of share repurchases under the right sets of conditions. But share repurchases are not a long-term replacement for top-line sales growth. And more than five years into an economic recovery, top line sales growth is still pretty lukewarm at best.,

I'm not at all opposed to investing in stocks, even at today's elevated valuations, so long as I remain tactical and willing to sell when the market finally cracks. But that's the key. This is not a "buy-and-hold" market. It's a market in which it pays to be cautious, stay tactical, and take the opportunities as they come.

Armed with the information in this book, you cannot only survive the most dangerous market in a generation, but you could be one of the few that prosper. Few saw the financial tsunami coming last time and the next will be no different. However, those that are prepared will flourish, while those that are not will endure tremendous financial and personal hardship. Your financial well-being and ultimately your way of life depend on you being properly equipped to surf the tsunami in front of you.

APPENDIX

Appendix A: An Economic Tsunami Lies Ahead—Prepare For This Perfect Storm; Your Way of Life Depends on It!

This section was originally published as a special report to Springer Financial Advisors clients and a warning to all in December of 2007—just months before the onset of the 2008 crisis and meltdown. Though now a little dated, I include this to give a sense of perspective. After a fantastic six year bull market, it's easy to get complacent and to forget how quickly an entire life's worth of saving and investing can disappear in an instant without the right kind of planning.

The original charts have been removed because they have already been discussed at length in the main body of the book.

America is at a crossroads. The convergence of economic fundamentals, market cycles, and demographic trends threatens the long-term economic prosperity to which we Americans have become accustomed. With Baby Boomers passing their peak spending years, a record number of Americans retiring and a government in crisis over how to pay for it, a storm of epic proportions is brewing. Few will see it coming, but those who are prepared may prosper, while those who are not will endure tremendous financial and personal hardship. Your financial well-being and ultimately your way of life depend on being ready for this Perfect Storm, this Economic Tsunami.

Soon, the 78 million Baby Boomers will pass their peak spending years and head into retirement. It's an important time because America is a nation driven by consumer spending. Personal consumption, or what people do as consumers, represents over 70% of the nation's Gross Domestic Product (GDP) and consumer spending is the largest factor in our economic health. Boom times

SURFING THE RETIREMENT TSUNAMI

are associated with an increasing size of the mid-forties population, because this is the age people spend the most, and bust times are associated with a decreasing size of this population. As larger groups of consumers reach an age when they spend more, the economy grows. In turn, when these groups pass their peak spending years, the economy slows—dramatically.

People spend money in predictable patterns at predictable times in their lives. These spending patterns directly impact our economy, business and product trends. They affect everything from the demand for potato chips and real estate to inflation rates, economic growth, immigration rates and domestic migration. By analyzing this information we can forecast how spending will change in the years and decades to come. Economists will continue to fret about the "over-extended" consumers and the dire consequences to come, however the boom in consumer spending will continue until Baby Boomers see their children finish their high school years and move out. How do we know all this? Demographics!

Demographics—The Ultimate Forecasting Tool

Demographic data categorizes consumers by age, income, lifestyles—even zip codes and neighborhood blocks. It predicts what new generations of consumers will do as they age, and it can help us see key trends that will affect our future. The life insurance industry was the first to use this data for actuarial predictions and risk assessment.

An economic boom is not just created by the rise of spending (demand), but also the simultaneous rise of productivity (supply) from an efficient maturing generation. This generates rising stock prices from higher earnings and rising valuations, along with low inflation. When older people leave the workforce, they are replaced with a younger, less efficient workforce, which leads to decreasing productivity with increasing inflation. The next cycle occurs once the spenders are gone, leading to decreasing prices for goods and services causing deflation.

People do predictable things as they age. Between ages 18 and 47, we go through several stages of life. From just entering the workforce at ages 18 to 22, and getting married between ages 22 and 30, the spending cycle is accelerated. Once children enter the picture, we typically then purchase our first home between ages 31 and 42. This is the stage at which we incur the most debt—and buy the most potato chips for ravenous 14-year-olds. Our spending continues to increase as we purchase our next home, more furnishings and cars, etc., until about age 47, as our kids reach their late teenage years and are still living in the household.

As we reach 50, the kids leave home. At this point, apart from that dream car at 54 and the expensive wine at 56, we begin to spend less, pay down debts and save more for retirement. Income doesn't decrease, but investment usually does. The peak rate of investment generally occurs at age 54, which continues into retirement at around age 63. Net worth typically peaks just after age of death, currently 78. With quantifiable data on all of the key things we do as we age, trends are largely predictable decades into the future.

Consider the events that looked like they would seriously derail the economy, but didn't—September 11, Hurricane Katrina and the Afghanistan and Iraq Wars, to name a few. How did we go through these incredible obstacles and yet spend more? These disasters and threats are not what we base our spending decisions on. Families have needs that must be taken care of regardless of the current market conditions. As we move through stages of life, we change our spending in very predictable ways. To better understand these dynamics, we must look at the Adjusted Birth Index.

Spending cycles can be forecasted by moving forward the birth index (adjusted for immigration) by the appropriate number of years to correlate with the size of the late forties population. If we plot the size of the late 40s age group with the projected year, we see the rising trend of peaks and troughs in spending due to past variations in birth and immigration rates. For example, fewer babies were born during the Great Depression. Thus, we would expect that 48 years later (during the 1970s) there would be fewer middle-aged people, thus the stagnation of the 1970's economy. Generation X (the Baby Boomers' children) are barely 1/3 the size of the Baby

Boomer generation (1946-1964). From this we bear witness to a very alarming fact; there just physically are not enough people in Generation X to keep up the pace of spending set by the Baby Boomers!

When the massive Baby Boomer generation finally passes its peak spending years, spending will slow, earnings will decline and stock valuations will fall dramatically. We have already seen this effect on real estate, which likely will not rebound until 2012-2015 when the Echo Boomers begin to buy their first homes. There are just not enough people to absorb the homes of the current generation. To make matters even worse, retiring boomers will be living off of their assets and subsequently selling assets in a declining market, forcing them to sell more to just to get the same amount of money. Add in a Social Security and Medicare system stretched beyond their breaking points to service this swell of retirees, and the government will be forced to raise taxes regardless of who is in the White House... A perfect storm.

Why does this matter?

In managing your finances, it is important to have a reasonable idea of what your expenses will be, especially in retirement. How will economic and demographic trends and inflation affect those expenses? A financial plan that assumes rising consumer prices will look very different from one that assumes stagnant or falling prices. A portfolio of bonds and cash would be decimated by a period of prolonged inflation, but it would be very profitable during a deflationary period. On the other hand, a portfolio of stocks and commodities should do relatively well in keeping pace with inflation but would be catastrophic during a period of deflation. Naturally, having a viable economic forecast that takes these factors into account is an essential part of building your financial plan.

The single most important financial decision you will make in the next 10 years will be your money management style and the asset allocation you choose as economic cycles shift. Choose well and you will be able to enjoy the products and services you buy at a lower cost, while watching your nest egg grow. Choose poorly and your nest egg will shrink and you will see your purchasing power erode. In the ensuing bear market, millions of Americans will lose their life savings—don't be one of them.

In Conclusion

I like to believe that I am optimist in both life and the American way. I believe America is the greatest nation the world has ever known, and there is nothing in our future we cannot achieve. Naturally, I hope some of my predictions are wrong, but we simply cannot take that chance and not be prepared. Headlines can shock you but they do not move markets in the long term. Terrorism is the newest phenomenon that we will have to deal with that our forefathers didn't, and we will. What I am certain about is that as powerful as wars, natural disasters and oil and gold spikes might be, the demographic spending cycle will continue to dominate the economy. With the end of the Baby Boom upon us, it is critical that you know how to invest to get the best returns, but with the least risk possible. Regardless of the economic conditions, I will be ready, and now so will you. **"Invest for need, not for greed!"**™

KEITH SPRINGER

Keith Springer is the author of Facing Goliath: How to Triumph in the Dangerous Market Ahead, host of Smart Money with Keith Springer on News Radio KFBK, and a frequent contributor on CNBC, FOX, Fortune, The Wall Street Journal and many more. He is also President and founder of Springer Financial Advisors in Sacramento, CA, and has been providing professional investment and retirement advice for more than 31 years.

Keith Springer began his career in 1985 at Merrill Lynch in his hometown of Boston, Massachusetts. In 1990, he tired of shoveling snow and moved to sunny California to study advanced portfolio management and investment management studies. In 1996, he became an independent Registered Investment Advisor and formed Springer Financial where he continues to serve as president today. Keith Springer lives in Sacramento with his son Josh, who is currently studying business and finance at Chico State University. Keith can be reached at 916-925-8900 or www.KeithSpringer.com.

NOTES

Paul McCulley, "The Liquidity Conundrum" CFA Institute Conference Proceedings Quarterly, March 2008.

The role of the velocity can be best understood by looking at the Equation of Exchange, an integral part of the Quantity Theory of Money beloved by the monetarist school of thought:

$MV_T = P_T T$ where
M = money supply
V_T = velocity of money
P_T = price level at time T
T = aggregate real value of all transactions for the period

For a longer explanation, see *http://en.wikipedia.org/wiki/ Quantity_theory_of_money*.

Bill Bonner and Addison Wiggin, Financial Reckoning Day, 2003 See Biblical book of Ecclesiastes.

Reinhart and Rogoff also authored an academic paper by the same name that covers much of the same material, available for free on the Harvard Economics Department website: *http://www. economics.harvard.edu/files/faculty/51_This_Time_Is_Different. pdf*.

See *http://en.wikipedia.org/wiki/Strauss_and_Howe for a good* summary of their work.

See *http://en.wikipedia.org/wiki/Hyman_Minsky#Understanding_ Minsky.27s_Financial_Instability_Hypothesis.*

See Reinhart, Carmen M. and Kenneth S. Rogoff (2010). "Growth in a Time of Debt," American Economic Review, Vol. 100

No. 2, May 2010, 573-78.

http://terpconnect.umd.edu/~creinhar/Papers/RR%20Debt%20 and%20Growth-01-18%20NBER.pdf.

Ferguson, Niall. "Complexity and Collapse: Empires on the Edge of Chaos." Foreign Affairs, March/April 2010.

For a well-written account in digestible modern English, I recommend Financial Reckoning Day by William Bonner and Addison Wiggin (which was recently republished). Bonner and Wiggin devote an entire chapter to Law's scheme, and many of the precise figures used in this chapter were taken from their book.

For a longer account of the John Law fiasco, I recommend Extraordinary Popular Delusions and the Madness of Crowds by Charles Mackey.

Niall Ferguson, in his Ascent of Money, also gives a good telling of the unfortunate story.

The Five Stages were quoted directly from Niall Ferguson's The Ascent of Money, but Ferguson's original source was Charles Kindleberger's Manias, Panics, and Crashes, which was in turn largely based on the pioneering work of Hyman Minsky. I highly recommend all three authors.

From The Wealth of Nations, Book IV.
"Say's Law" is attributed to Jean-Baptiste Say (1767-1832), the noted French classical economist, and is a standard tenet of several schools of economic thought, including classical, neo-classical, supply-side, and Austrian.

DellaVigna and Pollet's paper is available at the University of California at Berkley website: *http://www.econ.berkeley. edu/~sdellavi/wp/attention.pdf.*

See Birchall, Jonathan. "Two Men and a Baby Business,"

Financial Times, April 6, 2010 *http://www.ft.com/cms/ s/0/17d97d70-41b3-11df-865a-00144feabdc0.html*.

See Simon, Bernard. "U.S. motorcycle sector extends decline." Financial Times, October 24, 2010 *http://www.ft.com/cms/s/0/653c974c-df9b-11df-bed9- 00144feabdc0.html*.

See "Oktobergloom," The Economist, October 7, 2010 http:// www.economist.com/node/17204871.

See Pignal, Stanley. "Dutch look at weeding out cannabis cafes," Financial Times, October 8, 2010 *http://www.ft.com/cms/ s/0/2cc0e802-d2fb-11df-9ae9-00144feabdc0.html*.

Timothy Cogley and Heather Royer. "The Baby Boom, the Baby Bust, and Asset Markets," Federal Reserve Board of San Francisco Economic Letter, June 26, 1998.

Levy, Leon. The Mind of Wall Street: A Legendary Financier on the Perils of Greed and the Mysteries of the Market, 2002.

Haberman, Clyde, "People behaving poorly may be the ones to save the state from the poorhouse," New York Times, December 2008.

Robbins, Gary. Estate taxes: An historical perspective, Backgrounder, January 16, 2004.

Hyman, David A. Medicare Meets Mephistopheles. New York: The Cato Institute, 2006.

Swerlick, Robert A. "Our Soviet Health System." Wall Street Journal, June 5, 2007.

"Sicko" Forbes, August 13, 2007.
Pauly, Mark V. "The Economics of Moral Hazard." The American Economic Review, Vol. 58, No. 3, Part 1 (Jun., 1968), pp. 531- 537.

Havighurst, Clark C. Health Care Choices. Washington, DC: The AEI Press, 1995.
For a general description of the LTCM story, see Lowenstein, Roger. When Genius Failed. Random House, 2003.

Kolman, Joel. "LTCM Speaks." *www.derivativesstrategy.com.*
Taleb, Nassim Nicholas. The Black Swan. Random House, 2007.

Montier, James. "Was It All Just A Bad Dream?" February 2010 GMO White Paper.
Tasker, Peter. "Why The Bulls Have Got It All Wrong With Commodities," Financial Times, June 10, 2010.

Brown, Josh. "An Investing Frankenstein," The Reformed Broker, October 8, 2014. *http://thereformedbroker.com/2014/10/08/an-investing-frankenstein/*